THE MONTESSORI TODDLER

A PARENT'S GUIDE TO RAISING
A CURIOUS AND RESPONSIBLE HUMAN BEING

SIMONE DAVIES

ILLUSTRATED BY
HIYOKO IMAI

WORKMAN PUBLISHING | NEW YORK

Library of Congress Cataloging-in-Publication Data is available.

ISBN 978-1-5235-0689-7

Design and illustrations by Hiyoko Imai

Author photo by Rubianca Han Simmelsgaard

Editing assistance by Alexis Wilson Briggs, alphaomegaconsulting.nl

Feelings and Needs chart reprinted with permission by Yoram Mosenzon, connecting2life.net

Workman Publishing Co., Inc.
225 Varick Street
New York, NY 10014-4381
workman.com

themontessorinotebook.com
hiyokoimai.com

Printed in China
First printing February 2019

10 9 8 7

This book is for Oliver and Emma.

I feel honored to be your mother.

You inspire me every day.

CONTENTS

CHAPTER ONE

INTRODUCTION

CHAPTER TWO

INTRODUCTION TO MONTESSORI

CHAPTER THREE

MONTESSORI ACTIVITIES FOR TODDLERS

CHAPTER FOUR

SETTING UP THE HOME

CHAPTER FIVE

RAISING A CURIOUS CHILD WHO FEELS SEEN AND HEARD

PART ONE

ENCOURAGING CURIOSITY IN OUR CHILD

PART TWO

ACCEPTING OUR CHILD FOR WHO THEY ARE

CHAPTER SIX

NURTURING COOPERATION AND RESPONSIBILITY IN OUR CHILD

PART ONE
CULTIVATING COOPERATION

PART TWO
SETTING LIMITS

CHAPTER SEVEN

PUTTING IT INTO PRACTICE

PART ONE
DAILY CARE

PART TWO
DEALING WITH CHANGES

PART THREE
USEFUL SKILLS FOR OUR TODDLERS TO LEARN

CHAPTER EIGHT

BEING THE ADULT

CHAPTER NINE

WORKING TOGETHER

CHAPTER TEN

WHAT'S NEXT

REAL STORIES

HOME TOURS AND QUOTES FROM MONTESSORI FAMILIES

APPENDIX

INTRODUCTION

1

LET'S CHANGE THE WAY WE SEE TODDLERS

Toddlers are misunderstood humans. People see toddlers as difficult. There are not many good examples of how to be with toddlers in a loving, patient, supportive way.

They start to walk, they start to explore, they're only just learning to communicate with words, and they don't have a whole lot of impulse control. They can't sit still easily in cafes and restaurants, they see an open space and start running, they have tantrums (often at the most inconvenient times and in the most inconvenient places), and they touch anything that looks interesting.

They get called "the terrible twos." They do not listen. They keep throwing everything. They won't sleep/eat/use the toilet.

When my children were small, it didn't feel right to get their cooperation with threats, bribes, and time-outs, yet it was difficult to find alternatives.

I heard a radio interview when my first child was very young. The guest talked about the negative effects of using time-outs as a punishment—it alienated the child when they needed support and made the child upset with the adult rather than helping the child make amends. I listened attentively for the guest to tell parents what to do instead, but the radio interview ended there. It's been my mission since then to find my own answers.

I entered a Montessori school for the first time as a new parent and instantly fell in love. The environment was so carefully prepared and inviting. The teachers were approachable and spoke to our baby (and us) with respect. We put our names on the waiting list for the school and joined the parent-toddler classes.

I learned so much about the Montessori approach in these classes and about toddlers. Toddlers thrive in an environment that challenges them; they seek to be understood, and they take in the world around them like sponges. I realized that I related easily to toddlers—I could see their perspective, and the way they learned fascinated me. I was lucky to start working as Ferne van Zyl's assistant in this classroom.

I did my Montessori training with the Association Montessori Internationale in 2004, and when life took us from Sydney to Amsterdam, I was surprised there weren't any Montessori parent-child classes in our new city. So I soon started my own school—Jacaranda Tree Montessori—where I lead parent-child classes, helping families see their toddler in a new way and helping them incorporate the Montessori approach in their homes.

I continue to love learning from the nearly one thousand toddlers and parents I've seen over the many years running these classes. I've participated in Positive Discipline teacher training and learned Nonviolent Communication. I continue to read innumerable books and articles, speak to teachers and parents, and listen to radio programs and podcasts. And I've learned from my own children, who have grown from toddlers to teenagers.

I want to share with you what I have learned. I want to translate the wisdom of Montessori into simple language that is easy to understand and that you can apply in your own home. By picking up this book, you have taken a step in your own journey toward finding another way to be with your toddler, whether or not your child will attend a Montessori school.

You will get the tools to work together with your child, to lead them, and to support them, especially when they are having a hard time. You'll learn how to set up your home to get rid of the chaos and to bring some calm to your family's life. To set up a "yes" space for your child to freely explore. And you'll discover how to create Montessori activities at home that are just right for toddlers.

This will not happen in one day. And you are not trying to re-create a Montessori classroom. You can start small—work with what you already have, put away some of the toys you already have so that you can rotate them, start to really observe the children as they follow their interests—and gradually you'll find yourself incorporating more and more Montessori ideas into your home and daily life.

I hope to show you that there is another, more peaceful way to be with your toddler. To help you plant the seeds to raise a curious and responsible human being. To work on a relationship with your child that you will continue to build upon for years. To put Dr. Montessori's philosophies into practice every day.

It's time for us to learn how to see through our toddler's eyes.

WHY I LOVE TODDLERS

Most Montessori teachers have a favorite age to work with. For me it is working with my toddler friends. People are often confused by this preference. Toddlers can be hard work, they are emotional, and they do not always listen to us.

I want to paint a new picture of the toddler.

Toddlers live in the present moment. Walking down the street with a toddler can be a delight. While we make lists in our heads of the errands we need to run and what we need to cook for dinner, they remain present and spot the weeds growing up from a crack in the pavement.

When we spend time with a toddler, they show us how to be present. They are focused on the here and now.

Toddlers pick things up effortlessly. Dr. Montessori observed that children under 6 years old take in everything without effort, just as a sponge soaks up water. She referred to this as the *absorbent mind.*

We don't have to sit down with a 1-year-old and teach them grammar or sentence structure. By the age of 3 they already have an amazing vocabulary and are learning how to construct simple sentences (and, for some, complicated paragraphs). Compare this with learning a language as an adult—it takes a lot of effort and work.

Toddlers are enormously capable. Often it is not until we have our own child that we realize how enormously capable they are from such a young age. As they approach 18 months old, they might start to notice that we are heading to Grandma's house well before we are there by recognizing things along the route. When they see an elephant in a book, they'll run over to find a toy elephant in a basket.

When we set up our homes to make them more accessible to our young children, they take on tasks with eagerness, capability, and delight. They wipe up spills, fetch a diaper for the baby, put their trash in the wastebasket, help us make food, and like to dress themselves.

One day a repairman came to fix something in our home. I'll never forget the look on his face when my daughter (then just under 2 years old) walked past him on the way to the bedroom, changed her clothes, put some wet clothes in the hamper, and walked off to play. Clearly he was surprised to see how much she was capable of doing for herself.

Toddlers are innocent. I don't think any toddler has a mean bone in their body. If they see someone playing with a toy, they may simply think, *I'd like to play with that toy right now* and take it from the other child. They may do something to get a reaction (*Let's drop this cup and see my parent's reaction*) or be frustrated that something did not go their way.

But they are not mean-spirited, spiteful, or vengeful. They are simply impulsive, following their every urge.

Toddlers do not hold grudges. Picture a toddler who wants to stay at the park when it's time to leave. They melt down. The tantrum may even last half an hour. But once they calm down (sometimes with help), they go back to being their cheerful, curious selves—unlike adults, who can wake up on the wrong side of the bed and be cranky all day.

Toddlers are also amazingly forgiving. Sometimes we do the wrong thing—we lose our temper, we forget a promise we made, or we just feel a bit out of sorts. When we apologize to our toddler, we are modeling how to make amends with someone, and they are quite likely to give us a big hug or surprise us with an especially kind word. When we have that solid base with our children, they look after us, just as we look after them.

Toddlers are authentic. I love spending time with toddlers because they are direct and honest. Their authenticity is infectious. They say what they mean. They wear their hearts on their sleeves.

Everyone who has spent time with a toddler knows they will point to someone on the bus and say loudly, "That person has no hair." We may sink down in our seat while our child shows no signs of embarrassment.

That same directness makes them very easy to be around. There are no mind games being played, no underlying motives, no politics at play.

They know how to be themselves. They don't doubt themselves. They do not judge others. We would do well to learn from them.

Note: When I refer to toddlers, I'm talking about children from around 1 to 3 years old.

WHAT WE NEED TO KNOW ABOUT TODDLERS

Toddlers need to say "no." One of the most important developmental phases a toddler passes through is the "crisis of self-affirmation." Between 18 months and 3 years, children realize that their identity is separate from their parents' and they begin to desire more autonomy. At the same time they begin to say "no," they begin to use the personal pronoun *I*.

This movement toward independence does not come easily. Some days they will push us away, wanting to do everything by themselves; other days they will refuse to do anything at all or will cling to us.

Toddlers need to move. Just as an animal does not like to be caged, our toddlers will not sit still for long. They want to keep mastering movement. Once standing, they move on to climbing and walking. Once walking, they want to run and to move heavy objects—the heavier the better. There is even a name for the desire to challenge themselves to the highest level by, for example, carrying big objects or moving heavy bags and furniture: *maximum effort*.

Toddlers need to explore and discover the world around them. The Montessori approach recommends that we accept this, set up our spaces for our child to safely explore, get them involved in daily life activities that involve all their senses, and allow them to explore the outdoors. Let them dig in the dirt, take off their shoes in the grass, splash in the water, and run in the rain.

Toddlers need freedom. This freedom will help them grow to be curious learners, to experience things for themselves, to make discoveries, and to feel they have control over themselves.

Toddlers need limits. These limits will keep them safe, teach them to respect others and their environment, and help them become responsible human beings. Limits also help the adult step in before a boundary has been crossed to avoid the all-too-familiar shouting, anger, and blame. The Montessori approach is neither permissive nor bossy. Instead, it teaches parents to be calm leaders for our children.

Toddlers need order and consistency. Toddlers prefer things to be exactly the same every day—the same routine, things in the same place, and the same rules. It helps them understand, make sense of their world, and know what to expect.

When limits are not consistent, toddlers will keep testing them to see what we decide today. If they find it works to nag or melt down, they will try again. This is called *intermittent reinforcement*.

If we understand this need, we can have more patience, more understanding. And when we aren't able to provide the same thing every day, we will be able to anticipate that they may need additional support. We won't think they are being silly; we'll be able to see from their perspective that it's not the way they were hoping it would be. We can offer them help to calm down and, once they're calm, help them find a solution.

Toddlers are not giving us a hard time. They are having a hard time. I love this idea (attributed to educator Jean Rosenberg in the *New York Times* article "Seeing Tantrums as Distress, Not Defiance"). When we realize their difficult behavior is actually a cry for help, we can ask ourselves, *How can I be of help right now?* We move from feeling attacked to searching for a way to be supportive.

Toddlers are impulsive. Their prefrontal cortex (the part of the brain that houses our self-control and decision-making centers) is still developing (and will be for another twenty years). This means we may need to guide them if they are climbing on the table again or grabbing something out of someone's hands, and be patient if they become emotional. I like to say, "We need to be their prefrontal cortex."

Toddlers need time to process what we are saying. Instead of repeatedly telling our child to put on their shoes, we can count to ten in our head to allow them time to process our request. Often, by the time we get to eight, we'll see them start to respond.

Toddlers need to communicate. Our children try to communicate with us in many ways. Babies gurgle and we can gurgle back; young toddlers will babble and we can show an interest in what they are saying; older toddlers love asking and answering questions; and we can give rich language, even to these young children, to absorb like a sponge.

Toddlers love mastery. Toddlers love to repeat skills until they master them. Observe them and notice what they are working to master. Usually it is something hard enough to be challenging but not so difficult that they give up. They'll repeat and repeat the process until they perfect it. Once they've mastered it, they move on.

Toddlers like to contribute and be part of the family. They seem to be more interested in the objects their parents use than they are in their toys. They really like to work alongside us as we prepare food, do the laundry, get ready for visitors, and the like. When we allow more time, set things up for success, and lower our expectations of the outcome, we teach our young child a lot about being a contributing member of the family. These are things that they will build on as they become schoolchildren and teenagers.

PARENTING THE MONTESSORI TODDLER

When I first came to Montessori, I confess, my interest might have been considered superficial. I was attracted to the Montessori environments and activities. And I wanted to provide beautiful, engaging materials and spaces for my own children. I was not wrong. It's the easiest place to start.

Years later, I see that Montessori really is a way of life. Even more than the activities or the spaces, Montessori has influenced the way I am with my children, the children who come to my classes, and the children I come in contact with in my daily life. It's about encouraging a child's curiosity, learning to really see and accept a child as they are, without judgment, and remaining connected with the child, even when we need to stop them from doing something they really want to do.

It's not difficult to apply Montessori practices at home, but it may be quite different from the way we were parented and the way others around us parent.

In a Montessori approach, we see the child as their own person on their own unique path. We support them as their guide and gentle leader. They aren't something to be molded into what we see as their potential or to make up for our own experiences or unfulfilled desires as a child.

As a gardener, we plant seeds, provide the right conditions, and give enough food, water, and light. We observe the seeds and adjust our care if needed. And we let them grow. This is how we can parent our children, too. This is the Montessori way. We are planting the seeds that are our toddlers, providing the right conditions for them, adjusting when needed, and watching them grow. The direction their lives take will be of their own making.

> "[T]he educators [including parents] behave as do good gardeners and cultivators toward their plants."
>
> —Dr. Maria Montessori, *The Formation of Man*

TODDLERS ARE BRILLIANT

What seems to be a lack of flexibility ("I can't eat breakfast without my favorite spoon!") **IS ACTUALLY** an expression of their strong sense of order.

What looks like a battle of wills **IS ACTUALLY** your toddler learning that things don't always go their way.

What looks like repeating the same annoying game over and over **IS ACTUALLY** the child trying to gain mastery.

What appears to be an explosive tantrum **IS ACTUALLY** the toddler saying, "I love you so much, I feel safe to release everything that I've been holding on to all day."

What seems to be intentionally going slowly to wind us up **IS ACTUALLY** them exploring everything in their path.

What can be super embarrassing to hear a toddler say in public **IS ACTUALLY** the child's inability to lie, a model of honesty.

What seems like another night of interrupted sleep **IS ACTUALLY** chubby little arms giving you a big squeeze in the middle of the night to express their pure love for you.

GETTING THE MOST OUT OF THIS BOOK

You can read this book from cover to cover. Or just open it at a page that interests you and find something practical that you can use today.

Sometimes figuring out where to start can be overwhelming. To help make it more manageable, I've included key questions at the end of each chapter to help you begin to incorporate Montessori into your home and daily life. There are boxes and lists throughout the book for easy reference. You will also find a useful chart in the appendix titled "Instead of This, Say That." You may wish to copy it and hang it somewhere as a reminder.

In addition to all of the Montessori wisdom, I also draw on many of the resources (books, podcasts, training courses) I have discovered over the years that complement the Montessori approach and help me be a kind and clear guide for the toddlers in my classes and for my own children.

Use this book as inspiration. In the end, the goal is not to do every single activity, or have a completely clutter-free space, or be a perfect parent; it is learning how to see and support our toddlers. To have fun being with them. To help them when they are having a hard time. And to remember to smile when we start taking it all too seriously. It's a journey, not a destination.

INTRODUCTION TO MONTESSORI

2

A BRIEF HISTORY OF MONTESSORI

Dr. Maria Montessori was one of the first female doctors in Italy in the late 1800s. She worked at a clinic in Rome, tending to the poor and their children. She not only treated her patients' health but also provided them with care and clothing.

In an asylum in Rome, she observed children with emotional and mental disabilities who were sensorially deprived in their environment. In one case, she noticed that they were picking up crumbs—not to eat, but to stimulate their sense of touch. She proposed that education, not medicine, was the answer for these children.

Dr. Montessori did not begin with any preconceived methodology. Instead, she applied the same objective and scientific observation practices from her medical training to see what engaged the children, to understand how they learned and how she could facilitate their learning.

She immersed herself in educational philosophy, psychology, and anthropology, experimenting with and refining educational materials for these children. Eventually, the majority of the children passed state examinations with marks higher than children without disabilities. Dr. Montessori was hailed as a miracle worker.

She was soon able to test her ideas in the Italian educational system when she was invited to set up a place in the slums of Rome to care for young children while their parents worked. This was the first Casa dei Bambini—House of Children—which opened in January 1907.

It was not long before her work drew interest and spread internationally. Montessori schools and training programs are now on every continent except Antarctica. In the United States alone, there are more than 4,500 Montessori schools, and there are 20,000 worldwide. Where I live in Amsterdam, there are more than 20 Montessori schools for a population of around 800,000 catering to children from infancy to 18 years old. Larry Page and Sergey Brin (founders of Google), Jeff Bezos (founder of Amazon), Jacqueline Kennedy Onassis (former first lady), and Gabriel García Márquez (Nobel Prize–winning novelist) all attended Montessori schools.

Dr. Montessori continued to work in education and develop her ideas for children of all ages as she moved around the world—including living in India in exile during World War II—until her death in 1952 in the Netherlands. She called her work "an education for life"—i.e., not just for the classroom, but for our daily lives.

TRADITIONAL EDUCATION vs MONTESSORI EDUCATION

In traditional education, the teacher generally stands at the front of the classroom, decides what the children need to learn, and teaches the children what they need to know: a top-down approach.

It is also a one-size-fits-all approach. The teacher decides that everyone is ready to learn, for example, the letter *a* on the same day.

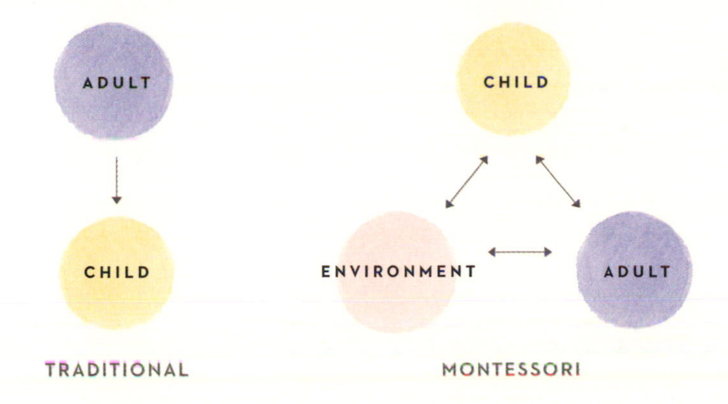

In Montessori education there is a dynamic relationship between the child, the adult, and the learning environment. The child is in charge of their own learning, supported by the adult and the environment.

The materials are laid out on shelves in a sequential order from easiest to hardest. Each child works at their own pace through the materials, following their interest in that moment. The teacher will observe the child and when it seems that the child has mastered the material, the teacher will then give them a lesson with the next material.

In the diagram of Montessori education above, the arrows are pointing in both directions. The environment and child interact with each other. The environment attracts the child and the child learns from the materials in the environment. The adult and environment are also affecting each other. The adult prepares the environment, observes, and makes adjustments where necessary to meet the child's needs. And the adult and child have a dynamic relationship, based on mutual respect for each other. The adult will observe the child and step in to give only as much assistance as necessary before stepping out of the way for the child to continue their self-mastery.

In her writing, Dr. Montessori reiterates that the objective of Montessori education is **not to fill a child with facts, but to cultivate their own natural desire to learn**.

These principles do not just apply in the classroom—they inform the way we are with our children in the home. We support our children to make discoveries for themselves, we give them freedom and limits, and we enable success by setting up our homes so they can take part in our daily lives.

SOME MONTESSORI PRINCIPLES

1. Prepared environment

I run eight classes a week at Jacaranda Tree Montessori. Much of my "work" is done before the children arrive. I prepare the environment with a lot of care and attention.

- I set up activities that are just the right level for the children—challenging to master but not so difficult that they will give up.
- I make sure the children have the tools they need to succeed—I look for trays they can carry, cloths at the ready to wipe up spills, a supply of art materials so they can practice and repeat, child-sized implements like spreaders for putting toppings onto crackers, and the smallest of glasses for drinking.
- I sit on the floor to see what it looks like from their height. I place artwork for them to enjoy low on the walls and plants for them to look after on the floor or on low tables.
- I prepare the space so it is simple and beautiful. I remove any clutter, I set out a few, well-chosen activities, and I make sure that activities are complete and not missing any parts so the children can work with them independently.

This never feels like "cleaning the classroom." The purpose of this preparation is to make things as attractive to them as possible and to allow the children freedom to explore and learn.

A prepared environment can be any space that we set up for our children: a classroom, our home, a holiday rental, an outside space.

2. Natural desire to learn

Dr. Montessori recognized that children have an intrinsic motivation to learn. Babies learn to grasp for an object, they learn to stand by trying again and again and again, and they master walking—all by themselves, within a supportive environment. The same applies to learning to talk, learning to read and write, learning mathematics, and learning about the world around them.

The discoveries children make for themselves—particularly within a *prepared environment*—build wonder in the child and a love of learning. They do not need to be directed to explore the environment.

In a Montessori classroom, the ages of the children are mixed. Younger children can learn from observing older children, and older children can consolidate their learning by helping the younger ones.

A toddler's work is play. They are intrinsically curious learners—if we allow them to be.

3. Hands-on, concrete learning

> "We may put it like this: the child's intelligence can develop to a certain level without the help of the hand. But if it develops with his hand, then the level it reaches is higher, and the child's character is stronger."
>
> —Dr. Maria Montessori, *The Absorbent Mind*

The hand takes in information in a concrete way to pass on to the brain. It's one thing to hear or watch something, but we learn on a deeper level when we integrate our listening or watching with using our hands. We move from passively learning to actively learning.

The materials in a Montessori classroom are so beautifully prepared and attractive that the child is drawn to them to make discoveries for themselves, **with their hands**.

We give toddlers tactile learning experiences. They hold an object as we name it, we offer a variety of beautiful art materials for them to explore, we provide interesting fastenings to open and close (from Velcro to zippers to buttons), and they help us prepare food in the kitchen—digging their fingers into the dough or using a butter knife to cut a banana.

Another example of hands-on learning is the math materials found in a Montessori classroom for 3-to-6-year-olds. A small golden bead represents 1. A string of 10 beads represents 10. A mat of 10 rows of 10 beads represents 100. A stack of 10 mats represents 1,000.

Using these materials, a young child can then do addition. For the sum 1,234 + 6,432, the child can go and get one 1,000 block, 2 mats for 100, 3 strings for 30, and 4 single beads. They can then do the same for 6,432. It is then very clear when they start adding that there are now 7 of the 1,000 blocks, 6 of the 100 mats, and so on. The child can concretely see and hold in their hands these values, unlike the abstract way in which most children learn addition on a piece of paper.

As the child moves into the upper elementary grades, they will be able to draw on this concrete base to move to abstraction. They will not need the materials, yet they are always available to them should they wish to revisit them.

4. Sensitive periods

When a child shows a particular interest in one area—for example, movement, language, math, reading—it is known as a *sensitive period*. This describes a moment when the child is particularly attuned to learning a certain skill or concept and it happens with ease and without effort.

We can watch our children to see what sensitive periods they are in and provide appropriate activities to encourage those interests.

When the toddler starts to mimic us—parroting certain words—we know they are in a sensitive period for language, and we can focus on giving the child new and familiar vocabulary for them to practice.

If a toddler is interested in climbing on the table, they are likely in a sensitive period for movement and need to practice those skills. Instead of allowing them to climb on furniture, we can create an obstacle course with pillows, blankets, things to balance on, and things to climb.

The table on the following page provides some examples of how we can feed our child's interest when they are in a sensitive period.

Note: Some people are worried that if they miss a sensitive period—for example, for reading—then the child will have problems learning to read. They will learn to read, but it will take more conscious effort, similar to an adult learning a foreign language.

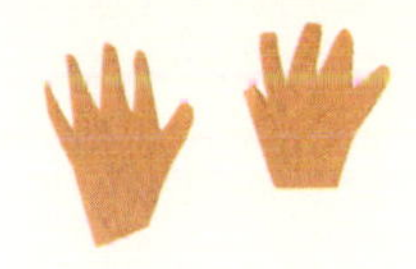

SENSITIVE PERIODS FOR TODDLERS

The exact timing of these sensitive periods is unique to each child.

LANGUAGE	A sensitive period for spoken language. They watch our mouth, they babble, they start parroting what we say, and soon afterward, there is a language explosion. An interest in writing may begin from 3.5+ years; reading from 4.5+ years. • Use rich language. • Name everything with its proper name. • Read books. • Have conversations with the toddler—allow pauses for them to react. • Follow the child's interests.
ORDER	Toddlers love order. Dr. Montessori observed a child out walking with her mother, who became very upset when her mother took off her coat. The child was upset because the "order" (how things were) changed and, when the mother replaced the coat, the child calmed down. • Use routines so the child knows what to expect next. • Have "a place for everything and everything in its place." • Provide understanding if the child is upset when something doesn't happen the same way every day.
TINY DETAIL	From 18 months to 3 years, the child is attracted to the smallest objects and the minutest detail. • Provide exquisite details in the home: art, flowers, handmade crafts. • Sit on the ground at their height to see what they can see from their perspective—make it attractive. • We can remove imperfect items.
MOVEMENT ACQUISITION	The young toddler acquires gross- and fine-motor movement—they learn to walk and to use their hands. The older toddler refines these skills and begins to develop more coordination. • Offer different opportunities for them to practice gross- and fine-motor movements. • Allow time for movement.
SENSORIAL EXPLORATION	Toddlers are fascinated by color, taste, smells, touch, and sounds through exploration of the environment. The older toddler begins to classify and organize these impressions. • Give access to a rich indoor and outdoor environment to be explored with all the senses. • Provide time to explore freely. • Make discoveries together.
MANNERS AND COURTESIES	The sensitive period for manners starts around 2.5 years. Before this, the adult can model manners and courtesies for young toddlers, who will absorb them. • Trust in the child that these manners and courtesies will gradually develop without haranguing the child to use them. • Model manners and courtesies in the home, in daily life, and with strangers.

5. Unconscious absorbent mind

From birth until about the age of 6, children take in information effortlessly. Dr. Montessori referred to this as the *absorbent mind*. From birth to the age of 3, they do this completely *unconsciously*.

The ease with which a toddler learns gives us opportunities as well as responsibilities.

Opportunities because they absorb with such ease the language around them (building a rich vocabulary and understanding), how we handle furniture and objects (ideally with care), how we treat others (ideally with respect and kindness), where we put things (creating order), and the beauty of the environment around them.

Responsibilities because, as Dr. Montessori points out, a sponge can absorb dirty water as easily as it can clean water. A child will pick up negative experiences as easily as positive experiences. They can even pick up our feelings and attitudes, for example, when we drop something and get frustrated with ourselves (as opposed to forgiving ourselves) or if we have a fixed mind-set that we are bad at drawing (as opposed to a growth mind-set where we might show that we can always keep improving our skills).

We can therefore be mindful, as much as possible, to be positive role models for our young children, to provide beauty, and to offer kindness for them to absorb.

6. Freedom and limits

I've heard people say, "Aren't Montessori schools really hands-off and the children can do whatever they like?" And I've heard others say, "Aren't Montessori schools really strict and the children are allowed to use materials only in certain ways?"

Montessori actually falls in the middle, somewhere between permissiveness and autocracy/dictatorship.

At school or at home, we can have a few rules for children to live by to learn respect and responsibility for themselves, others, and the environment around them. Within these limits, children have freedom of choice, of movement, and of will.

In a Montessori school, the children have the freedom to choose what they would like to work on (as long as it is available), the freedom to rest or to observe another child (as long as they are not disturbing another child), and the freedom to move around the classroom (as long as they respect the people around them). Within these limits, we follow the child and trust they will develop on their own unique timeline.

At home, we can give them freedom to choose what they want to wear (as long as it's appropriate for the season), the freedom to make their own snack (as long as they sit down to eat), and the freedom to express themselves (as long as they do not hurt others or objects in the home).

Some people worry, *How will they ever learn that there are some things they have to do?* or *Won't they become spoiled if we focus on them all the time?* I am not suggesting that we give our children license to do whatever they want. As parents we can be clear about what is expected and follow through with loving limits when necessary. We will step in if they are hurting someone or themselves, or we will gently help them leave the park if they are having trouble leaving themselves. And while we are learning to see from their perspective, we are also showing them how to have mutual respect and care for others (including us, as their parents) and the environment.

We give them freedom within limits.

7. Independence and responsibility

"Help me to help myself."

In Montessori, children learn to become remarkably independent. We don't do this so that children will grow up as fast as possible. (Let children be children.) We do this because children love it.

Children want to be able to do more, to contribute, to be a part of the family/classroom/society. We see satisfaction on their face when they pull on their own shoe, put something back where it belongs, or help a friend. Peace washes over them when they can do it for themselves, when they do not have to fight someone putting their T-shirt over their head for them or plopping them into the bath without warning.

Through independence the child learns **how to be responsible** for caring for themselves, others, and the environment.

They learn how to handle fragile things with care. They learn how to offer help to a friend. They learn how to take care of their belongings. They learn how to make amends when they have hurt someone. They learn how to look after the plants, the classroom, and the environment around them.

Even toddlers.

8. Individual development

Each child is on their own unique developmental timeline.

Montessori respects not only each child's unique timeline but also the fact that each child has different energy levels and is able to focus at different moments. Children have different modalities for learning—visual, aural, tactile, or a combination.

Some children like to repeat and repeat until they master a skill. Other children will learn mostly through observing others. Some children need to move more than others.

Montessori respects how different children learn, and supports their individual development.

9. Respect

A Montessori teacher will have such respect for the child that they will treat them the same way they would an adult. We can see this in the way they speak to the child, the way they ask permission if they need to touch them (for example, "Would it be okay for me to lift you up?"), and the way they allow the child to develop in their own way.

This does not mean that the adult is not in charge. They will set a limit when needed. Not passive. Not aggressive. But in a respectfully assertive way.

10. Observation

Observation is the basis of the Montessori approach. As part of my Montessori training, we observed babies and young children for 250+ hours. We were training ourselves to unlearn the desire to analyze, jump to conclusions, have biases, and form preconceptions about a child or a situation.

Observing simply means watching like a camera on the wall. Being factual, and recording only what we see: the children's movements, their language, their posture, their actions.

Observing shows us exactly where the child is right now. It helps us see what they are interested in, what they are working to master, when there is a developmental change, and, on occasion, when to step in to set a limit or to provide a little help before stepping out again.

TO PRACTICE

1. Do we see our child displaying any of the sensitive periods? What are they showing interest in right now?
2. Do we see examples in our child of:
   - the absorbent mind?
   - their natural desire to learn?
3. How do we feel about top-down learning (a traditional learning approach) versus an approach where the child is engaged in their own learning?

In the following chapters, I will show how to incorporate these Montessori principles into daily life:

- Observing our children to see what interests they have that they can explore and make discoveries about for themselves
- Providing time for language, movement, and being together
- Setting up our home so they can be successful
- Including them in daily life
- Encouraging their curiosity
- Setting a few ground/house rules so children know the limits
- Being our children's guide—because they don't need a boss or a servant
- Letting them blossom into the unique beings they are—instead of molding them

Let's put this into practice with our toddlers.

MONTESSORI ACTIVITIES FOR TODDLERS

3

MONTESSORI ACTIVITIES FOR THE WHOLE CHILD

Often the easiest way to begin with Montessori at home is to start with activities.

Montessori activities are based on developing the whole child. We begin by looking at the child to see what their needs are. We then set up activities to meet those needs.

Toddlers' needs consist of using their hands in various ways (working on their grasp, the ability to reach across the middle of their body, hand-to-hand transfer, carrying objects, using two hands together); practicing gross-motor movement; self-expression; and communication.

Montessori activities for toddlers fall into five main areas:

1. eye-hand coordination
2. music and movement
3. practical life (activities of daily life)
4. arts and crafts
5. language

There is a list of Montessori activities for toddlers in the appendix of this book. Ages are given as an indication only. Be sure to follow the child and see which activities keep their attention, removing those that are too hard or too easy.

WHAT MAKES AN ACTIVITY MONTESSORI?

Montessori activities usually **target one skill**. For example, putting a ball into a box through a small hole allows the child to master this one skill. This differs from many traditional plastic toys that target multiple skills at the same time, with one part for pushing, one part where a ball drops, another part that makes a noise, and so on.

We also prefer to use **natural materials**. Toddlers explore with all their senses. Natural materials like wood are lovely to touch and generally safe for putting in their mouths, and the weight of the object is more likely to be directly related to its size. Although they are sometimes more expensive, wooden toys are often more durable and can be found secondhand and then passed on once the child has finished with them. Storing activities in containers made of natural materials, like woven baskets, incorporates handmade elements and beauty into the space, too.

Many Montessori activities have **a beginning, middle, and end**. The child may begin with a small part of the sequence and, as they develop, will be able to complete the full *work cycle*, including replacing the activity on the shelf. They experience peace while they are practicing the activity—and satisfaction once they complete it. For example, when arranging flowers, at first a child may show interest only in pouring water and using the sponge to wipe it up. Gradually they will learn all the steps and complete the work cycle, filling small vases with water, arranging all the flowers, putting away the materials at the end, and cleaning up any water that was spilled.

Montessori activities are **complete**. Completing an activity is important for their sense of mastery. A child can become frustrated if, for example, a piece of a puzzle is missing. If any pieces are missing, we remove the whole activity.

Activities are often organized in individual **trays and baskets**. Within each tray or basket is everything the child needs to complete the task by themselves. For example, if the activity involves water, we may want to include a sponge or hand mitt to clean up any spills.

Children gain mastery of an activity through **repetition**. The activity should be exactly at their level—challenging enough that it is not too easy yet not so difficult that they give up. I love seeing a row of clothespins along the top of a painting on the drying rack—a sign that a child has been busy working to master pinning up their paintings to dry.

They may focus on and repeat just one part of the activity. For example, they may practice squeezing a sponge or filling a jug with water from a tap. We observe and allow them to repeat and repeat the section they are trying to master. They will eventually add steps to the process or move on to another activity.

A child has the **freedom to choose** an activity. Our spaces are set up to encourage this freedom of choice by displaying a limited number of activities that they are working to master.

> "The task of teaching becomes easy, since we do not need to choose what we shall teach, but should place all before him for the satisfaction of his mental appetite. He must have absolute freedom of choice, and then he requires nothing but repeated experiences which will become increasingly marked by interest and serious attention, during his acquisition of some desired knowledge."
>
> —Dr. Maria Montessori, *To Educate the Human Potential*

HOW TO SHOW THE CHILD AN ACTIVITY

In Montessori teacher training, we learn to show children how to do each activity in the classroom by giving them "a presentation." In a presentation, each activity is broken into little steps, from taking the tray to the table, to presenting the activity step by step, to returning the tray to the shelf. We practice the presentation for each activity over and over. Then, if the child needs help in class, we know the activity so well from practicing that we can improvise and step in to give them just as much help as they need.

We can use the same approach at home. We can set up an activity, do it ourselves first, break the activity into little steps, and practice to see how our child might manage.

Let them choose the activity they are interested in and try it for as long as they can without interfering. Even if they drop something, we can sit on our hands to see if they will react and pick it up themselves. When we see that they are struggling and getting frustrated, we can step in and say, "Watch," and then show them, slowly, for example, how to turn the lid of the jar. Then we can step back again to see how they manage.

Here are some tips for showing an activity to the child:

- Make precise, slow hand movements so the child can observe clearly. For example, break down all the tiny steps we take to open a button, and slowly show them each one.
- Avoid talking as we demonstrate—otherwise the child won't know whether to look at us while we talk or watch our hands.
- Try to show them the same way each time to make it easier for them to pick up any steps they may be missing.
- Handle the objects in a way that the child can manage, for example, using two hands to carry a tray, a glass, and so on.
- If they don't want us to help, they may be open to a verbal cue, like "Push, push." Or we can let them keep trying by themselves until they master the task. Or they may walk away and try again at another time.

S LOW
H ANDS
O MIT
W ORDS

I first heard the acronym *SHOW* from my Montessori friend Jeanne-Marie Paynel. It is a useful reminder to adults to use slow hands and omit words when we are showing our children something new.

This helps the child pick things up more easily. Our movements are slow and easy to follow. If we explain with words at the same time, our toddler isn't sure whether to listen to us or watch us—so we stay quiet so they can focus on our movements without words.

GENERAL PRINCIPLES TO KEEP IN MIND

1. Let the child lead

Follow the child's pace and interests. Let them take the time to choose for themselves rather than suggesting or leading the play. Let them pick from activities they are working to master—nothing too easy or too difficult. Something challenging but not so hard that they give up.

2. Let them work with the activity as long as they like

As the child is mastering an activity, we do not want to rush them to finish—even if a sibling is waiting. Once they have finished the activity, ask if they would like to do it again. This encourages repetition and gives them the chance to repeat, practice, master the activity, and increase their concentration.

Ideally, we don't interrupt our child's deep focus. A simple comment from us can distract them from whatever they are working to master, and they may abandon the activity completely. Wait until they look to us for feedback, step in to offer help when they are frustrated, or see that they have finished before we make a request like coming to the table to eat dinner.

3. Avoid quizzing the child

We may not realize we are doing it, but we are constantly quizzing our children. "What color is this?" "How many apples am I holding?" "Can you show Grandma how you can walk?"

I did it too when my son was small. Often I'd ask him to demonstrate some new skill or perform some new trick on cue. Maybe to show off in some way. Or maybe to push him to learn a little faster.

Now I see that this prompting is a kind of test for a child. And there is generally only one correct answer, so if the answer they give is wrong, we have no other option than to say, "No, that flower is yellow, not blue." Not exactly great for building a child's confidence.

Instead we can continue to name things, ask questions to arouse curiosity, and use observation to see what the child has mastered and what they are still practicing.

Now, the only time I will quiz a child is if I am 100 percent sure they know the answer and will be excited to tell me. For example, if they have been identifying blue objects all by themselves, I could point to something blue and ask, "What color is this?" They will be delighted to shriek, "Blue!" This usually starts when they are about 3 years old.

4. Put the activity away when finished

When the child is finished with an activity, we can encourage them to return it to its place on the shelf. This routine emphasizes that there is a beginning, middle, and end to a task.

And putting things back in their special place on the shelf gives order and calm to the space.

With young toddlers, we can first model where things belong and introduce putting things back as the last part of the activity. We can then start to work together with our child to bring things back to the shelf—they might carry one part and we carry the other. Then we can scaffold onto this base by encouraging them to put it back by themselves, for example, tapping the shelf where it belongs. Gradually we will see them put things away more and more by themselves.

They may not do this every day, just as we do not feel like cooking every day. Instead of insisting that they do, we could say, "You want me to do it? Okay, I'll carry this one and you carry that one."

Even older children may need some help breaking the task into manageable parts. "Let's first put the blocks back, and then we'll work on the books."

If they have moved on to the next activity, I do not generally break their concentration. Instead I put away the activity myself, modeling for the child what to do the next time. They may not actually see us do it, but they may see us from the corner of their eye or unconsciously absorb what we are doing.

5. Model, model, model

Our child learns a lot from observing us and other people around them. So we can think how a young child could be successful and model that—for example, push in our chair with two hands, avoid sitting on a low table or shelf, and carry just one thing at a time.

6. Allow any use of the materials, but stop when they're used inappropriately

A child will explore activities in different ways (and often in ways we weren't expecting). We do not want to limit their creativity by stepping in to correct them. If they are not harming the materials, themselves, or someone else, then there is no need to interrupt them. We could perhaps make a mental note to show them its purpose at another time. For example, if a child is using a watering can to fill a bucket, we could show them at another neutral moment how to use the watering can to water some plants.

However, if the child is using the objects inappropriately, we may gently step in. For example, "I can't let you bang that glass on the window." We could then show them that the glasses are for drinking or show them an activity that allows them to use that skill, for example, banging a drum or doing a small hammer-and-nail activity.

7. Modify to meet their level

We may be able to modify an activity to make it easier or more difficult. For example, if our child is struggling with putting shapes into a shape sorter, we can keep the easier shapes (like a cylinder) and remove the more difficult shapes. Then we can build up slowly, adding in a few more shapes as our child gains more skill.

Sometimes for a younger child, when there are fewer items in a set, the child's concentration increases. For example, in my classroom we usually have five to eight animals in our wooden barn, which gets used all the time. We can make more items available as the child grows.

8. Arrange the activities on shelves from easiest to hardest

By putting the activities on the shelf in increasing difficulty from left to right, we help the child move from easier to more difficult activities. If they find an activity too difficult, they can move back to the earlier activity.

9. Use what is available

There is no need to buy all the materials featured in this book. They are meant only to give an idea of the types of activities that will interest toddlers. Similar ones can be made from things we already have lying around the house.

Here are some examples:

- If our child is interested in how coins go into a slot, rather than buying a coin box, cut a narrow slot into a shoe box and offer some large buttons for the child to put through the hole.
- If our child is interested in threading, they can thread dried penne pasta onto a shoe lace with a large knot at the end.
- If our child is interested in opening and closing, collect old jars and rinse them out so our child can practice taking the lids on and off. Use old wallets or purses with different clasps. Hide some fun things inside for them to discover.

10. Be careful with small parts and sharp objects

Montessori activities often involve objects with small parts, or may involve knives or scissors. These activities should always be supervised. We don't need to hover—yet we keep observing in a calm way to make sure they are using the items in a safe way.

HOW TO SET UP AN ACTIVITY

Toddlers generally choose what to play with according to what looks interesting to them in the moment.

So, instead of simply placing an activity on the shelf, I recommend taking a couple of minutes to set it up in a way that makes it even more engaging for our child.

1. **Display it on a shelf.** Rather than storing activities in a toy box, it is much easier for a toddler to see what is available when we set a few things out on a shelf.

2. **Make it attractive.** Putting an activity into a basket or tray can make it more appealing to a child. If the child does not seem interested in the activity anymore, sometimes changing the tray can make it more appealing.

3. **Show what belongs together.** A tray or basket keeps all the necessary items together. For example, with a play-dough tray we can include a container of play dough; implements they can use to mold, cut, and make patterns; and a mat to protect the table.

4. **Prepare everything so our child can help themselves.** In a painting area, we can have the apron hanging on a hook off one side of the easel and a damp cloth hanging off the other side at the ready for spills, to wipe their hands, or to clean the easel at the end. There could be a basket of fresh paper so they can help themselves and a folding clothesline with clothespins so they can hang their paintings to dry by themselves. Younger children will need some help with these steps, but gradually they will be able to take on more and more themselves.

5. **Undo the activity.** A completed activity is less attractive to a toddler than one that has been left undone. Disassemble the activity before returning it to the shelf. Place the pieces in a bowl to the left (say, puzzle pieces) and the activity to the right (the empty puzzle base). Tracking the movement from left to right is indirect preparation for reading.

HOW TO SET UP AN ACTIVITY

EXAMPLES

ELEMENTS

- tray
- undone
- left to right
- easiest to hardest along shelf
- at child's height
- beautiful to attract child's interest
- challenging to child—not too easy, not too difficult
- everything at the ready
- items the child can manage themselves

NºI **WATERCOLOR**

On a tray:

- watercolor brush
- small jar with small amount of water
- watercolor tablet (begin with one color if you can find the colors separately, so the colors aren't mixed together)

Also provide:

- an underlay to protect the table
- watercolor paper (a little thicker than regular paper)
- a cloth for small spills

Nº2 **SETTING TABLE**

We can show our child how to set the table, providing the following:

- a real glass, small enough for a toddler to manage
- bowl or plate
- small fork, spoon (knife if your child is using one)

Also provide:

- a place mat with markings for fork, spoon, knife, bowl, and glass

TYPES OF ACTIVITIES

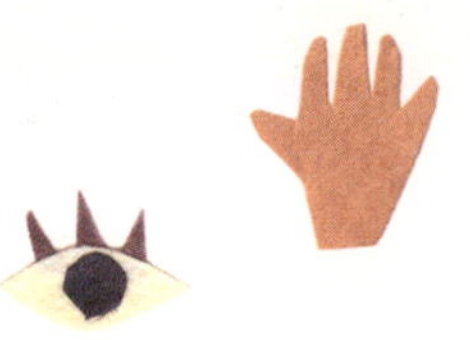

01 / EYE-HAND COORDINATION

Toddlers are constantly refining their grasp and practicing working with two hands together. Look for new ways to challenge these movements.

Threading activities

Threading allows our child to refine their grasp, eye-hand coordination, and dexterity, and provides practice working with two hands together.

- Up to 12 months, a baby will be able to remove large rings from a peg and start to replace them.
- Young toddlers can begin to sequence these rings in order from largest to smallest.
- There is also a version with three colored pegs (red, yellow, and blue) and three corresponding colored rings. At first the child is interested in putting the rings onto any peg. Eventually, they start to put a red ring on, say, the blue peg, stop, look for the red peg, and move the red ring to the red peg, matching the color.
- We can then offer ways for the child to thread a ring horizontally—instead of a vertical peg, we can make it horizontal. This introduces a movement called *crossing the midline*, where the child makes a movement with one hand from one side of their body to the other side across their midline.
- Then we move from threading to bead stringing. A good intermediary step is to first offer the child some beads and a wooden stick around 12 inches (30 cm) long.
- Next we can offer a shoelace with some beads. Look for threading sets where the shoelace has a wooden end on it around 1.5 inches (3–4 cm) long, which makes it easier for younger toddlers.
- Then we move on to stringing large beads onto a regular shoelace . . .
- . . . and then stringing smaller beads onto a thin shoelace.

Posting activities

With posting activities the child learns to release an object into a container and begins to understand object permanence (i.e., when something goes away, it can come back).

- Up to 12 months—a baby enjoys putting balls into a box or banging a ball through a hole with a hammer.
- Around 12 months—the young toddler moves on to pushing shapes through holes, starting with a cylinder. Then they can move on to more complex shapes such as a cube, triangular prism, and so on.
- With increasing dexterity the child can start inserting a large coin (or poker chip) into a narrow slot. In our class, inserting coins into a coin box with a key is one of the children's favorite activities.

Opening and closing activities

Another way to work a child's hands is to provide opportunities for them to open and close various containers.

- Use old purses with clasps, empty jars, containers with press stud fasteners, wallets with zippers, and so on. I hide different objects inside for the child to find—a small toy baby, a die, a spinning top, a key ring with the ring removed, etc.
- Find lockboxes where the child can open and close various locks (including a padlock with a key) to reveal small items hidden inside.

Pegboard and elastic bands; nuts and bolts

These activities are great ways to refine the child's fine-motor development.

- The child improves their coordination by stretching elastic bands over a pegboard.
- The child can screw a nut onto the bolt with one hand holding the bolt and the other turning the nut, allowing both hands to work together.
- Offer various sizes of nuts and bolts so the child can organize them by size.

Sorting

Starting around 18 months, toddlers become interested in sorting objects by color, type, and size. Supply a group of objects (or even better, find them with the child at the beach, in the forest, or in the garden). Place them in a large bowl to sort into smaller bowls. A container with compartments would also be perfect for a sorting activity. Some examples of good sorting objects:

- buttons in two or three different colors/sizes/shapes
- shells, two or three different kinds
- nuts in their shells, two or three different kinds

Stereognostic bags

Around 2.5 years, the child will be interested in figuring out what an object is simply by feeling it. Then begins the fun with stereognostic bags, more simply known as mystery bags. (*Stereognosis* is the ability to know an object by feeling around it.)

Find a bag (ideally one that is difficult to peek inside) and put a variety of objects inside. The child can put their hand in and guess what they feel, or we can name an item for them to feel for in the bag.

- Place inside the bag random objects *or* objects around a theme *or* paired objects with two of the same of each item.
- Choose objects that are distinctively shaped, like keys or spoons, rather than items like animals that are harder to distinguish.

Puzzles

Babies and young toddlers like pulling apart puzzles. Knob puzzles where the puzzle pieces fit into a designated shape are perfect for this age. By the time our child is around 18 months, they may be able to fit some simple shapes into the puzzle base.

- The young toddler can start with simple three-to-five-piece puzzles with large knobs. Even if the child is unable to put the pieces back, they are refining their fine-motor development. In this case, I would step in to model putting the pieces back so they can repeat the process of taking them out.
- From about 18 months, the child can move on to nine-piece puzzles with smaller knobs or no knobs.

- Jigsaw puzzles are the next step. Some look like a traditional puzzle with all the pieces the same size. Other puzzles are in the shape of an object—for example, the shape of a tree. The difficulty will depend on the number of pieces.

Note: Young children do not complete a jigsaw puzzle in the same way as an adult. Adults often find the corners and edges first. Children, on the other hand, tend to tackle the puzzle spatially, seeing which shapes fit together. When they are first starting to work on jigsaw puzzles, we can have a turn first to show them or give them two pieces at a time that fit together. They will gradually do more and more by themselves until they have mastered it.

02 / MUSIC AND MOVEMENT

Music

All humans need to move, and all cultures have a long history of singing and dancing. We don't have to be able to sing or play music well for children to enjoy music in the home. If we enjoy it, they will too. Making sounds with instruments, mimicking the rhythm our child makes, copying the movements they are making, or playing start-and-stop games are just as fun as singing along to a song.

Examples of musical instruments that are suitable for toddlers:

- Instruments to shake, such as maracas, tambourines, gourds, and shakers
- Instruments to strike with a mallet, such as a xylophone, drum, or tone block
- Instruments that you blow into, such as a harmonica or recorder
- Music boxes where we turn a handle to make a tune

Listening to music is its own activity. Even though they are a bit old-fashioned, a CD player or an old iPod (one that stores only music) allows a child to select music for themselves. We can even have a mat that they can unroll as a dancing mat.

Many children move instinctively when music comes on. A family may have traditional or cultural dances that they enjoy performing or watching. Spontaneous singing with actions is also fun, like singing along to "The Wheels on the Bus" or "Head, Shoulders, Knees, and Toes."

It is also lovely to take young children to concerts—many concert halls welcome young children or have special performances for children where they can look at the instruments at the end.

Movement

We can provide many movement opportunities for our children:

- running
- jumping
- skipping
- hopping
- brachiating (swinging like a monkey)
- biking
- climbing
- sliding
- balancing
- kicking and throwing balls

If possible, we can head outdoors for movement in the backyard, nearby forest, playground, town square, beach, mountain, river, or lake—even if the weather is not great. "There is no such thing as bad weather, just bad clothing," as the Scandinavians like to say. Living in the Netherlands, we put on our wet-weather clothes and cycle on.

We can also think about how to incorporate movement inside our home, space permitting. In my classroom we have a climbing wall. The young children start to pull up on the lower holds; as they get to around 2 years old, they climb with some support from an adult, and it is not long before they are able to hold their own weight and climb independently. Every muscle of their bodies is hard at work.

Children also like to hide, so think about creating spaces with blankets and chairs, hammocks, and tents. Overgrown gardens make fun hiding spots, too.

03 / PRACTICAL LIFE

ACTIVITIES OF DAILY LIFE AROUND THE HOME

Most parents notice that toddlers love to help around the home, participating in activities that have to do with looking after ourselves and our environment. These activities might be chores to us, but young children love them. And I should mention that they are great for calming active children.

Dr. Montessori discovered quickly that the children in her school wanted to help care for the classroom, themselves, their classmates, and the environment. So she introduced child-sized tools to help them succeed.

These activities are great for learning a sequence, like retrieving and putting on an apron all the way through washing and drying the dishes.

The task will go more slowly and require supervision when the child helps. We'll need to lower our expectations about the final product—the banana slices may be a bit mashed and the beans may have some ends that were missed. However, once they have mastered the skills, our child will become more and more independent. My children have grown up baking and cooking. Now that they are teenagers, they bake a lot and sometimes offer to cook dinner as well.

Here are some ways children can help around the home:

- **Plant care**—watering the plants, dusting the leaves, planting seeds, arranging flowers in small vases (using a small funnel and small pitcher to fill the vase with water)
- **Food preparation**—washing vegetables, beating eggs, scooping their own cereal out of a small container and adding milk from a small jug
- **Snack time**—helping themselves to food from an accessible snack area (which we restock daily with the help of our child, putting out only as much as we are happy for them to eat), peeling and slicing fruit, spreading topping on crackers, squeezing orange juice, pouring water to drink from a small jug
- **Mealtimes**—setting and clearing the table, washing dishes
- **Baking**—taking turns, measuring ingredients, helping to add ingredients, stirring
- **Cleaning**—sweeping, dusting, wiping spills, cleaning windows, polishing mirrors
- **Caring for pets**—feeding the pet, helping to walk the dog, filling up a water bowl

- **Learning to care for themselves**—blowing nose, brushing hair and teeth, washing hands
- **Dressing themselves**—taking socks on and off, fastening Velcro shoes, putting on a T-shirt, pulling trousers up and down, putting on a coat (see page 140 to learn the coat flip), practicing opening and closing zippers/snaps/buttons/shoelaces
- **Helping with the laundry**—bringing dirty clothes to the laundry basket, putting clothes in and taking them out of the washing machine, adding soap, sorting the clean clothes
- **Getting ready for overnight visitors**—making the beds, putting out a clean towel for the guests, putting away toys
- **Trips to the supermarket**—making a list with pictures, getting things from the shelves, helping to push the shopping cart, passing things to us to put on the checkout counter, carrying bags of groceries, putting groceries away at home
- **Volunteer work**—It's never too early to set the example of helping others. When my children were young, one of our weekly outings was to a local nursing home where we would visit the same residents each week. Seeing a young toddler and baby was the highlight of their week, and it taught my children at an early age that it feels lovely to help others.

Tips for practical life activities at home

Most of all, remember that it is meant to be fun. Stop before becoming overwhelmed. And keep practicing!

- Put out only as much as we want to clean up, be it water, dish soap, or a travel-sized bottle of shampoo.
- Have cleaning supplies at the ready: a hand mitt on the table to wipe up small spills, a child-sized broom and mop for larger spills.
- When children are younger than 2 years old, activities will likely have only 1 or 2 steps. As they gain mastery, add more steps (for example, put on an apron, wipe up at the end, take wet cloths to the laundry, and so on).
- Focus on the process, not the result. When the child helps, the task will take longer and the result may not look perfect, but the child is learning to master these skills and will become a lifelong helper at home.
- Look for ways the child can help. When they are younger, keep it simple (an 18-month-old can help carry the T-shirt while we carry the pants to the laundry basket and/or rinse some salad leaves for dinner); as they get to 2+ years, they can help out with even more.

- Look for baskets, trays, and simple caddies to arrange items for them to help, for example, to keep all the window-cleaning items together at the ready.
- We don't have to spend a lot of money. Keep it budget friendly by creating activities with things around the home. And look out for a few nice things like a wooden broom or a larger item like a learning tower to add to a list for birthdays and other special occasions.

Benefits of practical life activities at home

Beyond the simple pleasure young children take from these practical life activities, they are valuable in more ways than one:

- The child is learning to take responsibility in the home.
- We are working together to create, practice, and master the activities.
- Collaboration creates connection.
- These skills require repetition to gain mastery, which is great for building concentration.
- Our child enjoys feeling like a part of the family and being able to contribute.
- These activities involve sequences. As our child's concentration grows, we can increase the number of steps in the activity.
- These activities involve a lot of movement, great for refining fine-motor and gross-motor skills (for example, pouring water without spilling, using a sponge).
- There are many language opportunities around these activities: talking about what we're doing together and giving vocabulary for kitchen implements, food, tools for cleaning, and so on.
- The child learns new skills, independence, and a feeling of self-reliance.

I always say it is good to start young to lay a strong foundation while they are willing. These practical life skills help children learn to care for themselves, care for others (pets, for example), and care for their environment.

SOME AT-HOME PRACTICAL LIFE ACTIVITIES BY AGE

Wondering how to include your child around the home? Here are some ideas for various ages.

You can see how we scaffold their skills with these simple one-step activities for children from 12 to 18 months. Then, in addition to these activities, we offer activities of increasing difficulty for children from 18 months to 3 years. The child from 3 to 4 years old can begin longer, more complex tasks, in addition to those activities from earlier age groups.

12 to 18 months

KITCHEN

- Pour glass of water or milk using small jug—use small amount of liquid to avoid large spills
- Add milk to cereal
- Scoop cereal into bowl
- Wipe up spills with hand mitt
- Take plate to kitchen
- Drink from a glass

BATHROOM

- Brush hair
- Brush teeth with assistance
- Wash hands
- Pack away bath toys
- Fetch and hang up towel

BEDROOM

- Fetch diaper/underwear
- Put dirty clothes in laundry basket
- Open curtains
- Choose between two options for clothing
- Get dressed with assistance
- Take off socks

OTHER

- Help put toys away
- Fetch shoes
- Help the parent (for example, "Can you bring me the watering can, please?")
- Turn light switch on/off

18 months to 3 years

KITCHEN

- Prepare a snack/sandwich
- Peel and slice a banana
- Peel a mandarin orange
- Peel and cut an apple with assistance
- Wash fruits and vegetables
- Make orange juice
- Set the table/clear the table
- Wipe the table
- Sweep the floor—use a dustpan and brush
- Make coffee for parent (push buttons on coffee machine/fetch cup and saucer)

BATHROOM

- Blow nose
- Brush teeth
- Wash body—use small travel-sized soap bottles to minimize waste
- Clean face

BEDROOM

- Help to make bed by pulling up cover
- Choose clothes
- Get dressed with little help

OTHER

- Arrange flowers in small vases
- Pack and carry bag/backpack
- Put on coat
- Put on shoes with Velcro closure
- Water plants
- Put toys into baskets and return them to shelf
- Clean windows
- Load/unload washing machine and dryer
- Sort socks and clothing by color
- Fetch products in supermarket/push cart/help unpack groceries
- Dust
- Put leash on dog and brush dog

3 to 4 years

KITCHEN

- Unload dishwasher
- Measure and mix ingredients for baking
- Scrub and peel vegetables, such as potatoes and carrots
- Assist with cooking (for example, making lasagna)

BATHROOM

- Use toilet/flush toilet/close toilet seat
- Place wet clothing in laundry area
- Wipe with assistance after using toilet
- Wash hair—use travel-sized bottles to minimize waste

BEDROOM

- Make bed—pull up duvet
- Pack clothes into drawers/closet

OTHER

- Feed pets
- Help with recycling
- Fold laundry
- Fold socks
- Vacuum
- Open car door with remote

04 / ARTS AND CRAFTS

Dr. Montessori was asked if the Montessori environment produced good artists. Her response: "I don't know if we produce good artists. But we do produce a child with an eye that sees, a soul that feels, and a hand that obeys." For toddlers, arts and crafts activities are about self-expression, movement, and experiencing different materials. **The process takes precedence over the product.**

Types of arts and crafts activities:

- For young toddlers, we start with drawing. Look for crayons or pencils that glide easily on the paper. Chunky pencils are generally easier for a young toddler to grip, and produce more color than a regular color pencil. Crayons made of natural materials like beeswax or soy are lovely to draw with.
- We can then add a watercolor activity. I like to start with one or two colors at first. If we add more colors, everything tends to turn brown. The tray can contain a very small jar for holding water (little jam jars from hotels are the perfect size), a watercolor brush, and a dish with the watercolor tablet/s. We can have a piece of paper on an underlay (to protect the table), more paper if they would like to repeat, and a cloth at the ready for spills.
- We can introduce using scissors (with supervision) from around 18 months. For the cutting work, use real scissors with rounded ends that cut well, and show the child how to use them appropriately. We can show them we sit down at the table to use them and hold the handles, not the blades. Offer small strips of paper, which will be easier to snip. The pieces can then be collected into a small envelope and closed with a sticker.
- Around 18 months, a gluing activity can be great fun and help them refine their movements by using a small brush with a pot of glue (or a glue stick) to apply glue to the back of the shape and stick it onto the paper.
- Paint and chalk are also fun for toddlers. For younger toddlers, we may wish to only put out paint when we are able to supervise. Again, have wet cloths at the ready for wiping hands, the floor, or the board.
- Clay, play dough, and kinetic sand are lovely creative mediums for toddlers. We can add some simple tools like a rolling pin, cookie cutters, a blunt knife, or shaping tools to manipulate the material in many ways. I love making play dough with them, too. (See page 234 for my favorite recipe for homemade play dough.)

- Around 2.5 years, we can offer simple sewing activities. The sewing box can contain a needle case with a blunt darning needle, some thread, and a 4" x 4" (10 cm x 10 cm) cardboard square with holes punched along the diagonal.
- Short visits to museums help cultivate an appreciation of art. At the museum, we can look for colors, textures, and animals. We can play simple games, like selecting a postcard from the museum shop and then looking for the painting in the gallery.

Tips for arts and crafts

1. Try not to be prescriptive. Rather than showing a child what to make with the art materials, we show them how to use the materials and leave the experimentation up to them. For this reason, Montessori teachers prefer not to use coloring books because of the suggestion that children need to stay within the lines. Similarly we try not to limit children to using only green for grass and blue for sky. They can be creative in their choices.

2. Give feedback. In Montessori, rather than tell the child their artwork is "good" we like to leave it up to the child to decide if they like what they have made.

Instead we can give feedback and encouragement. We can describe what we see; for example, "I see you made a line over here in yellow." This can be more meaningful than saying, "Good job." Then the child really knows what we appreciate when we are looking at their work.

Also, because toddlers are mostly still just making movements of self-expression, we can ask, "Would you like to tell me about your painting?" rather than "What is it?" It may not be a picture of anything in particular but may simply be an expression of the movements in their body.

3. Use good-quality materials. I always recommend quality over quantity, which is particularly important when working with art materials. I would rather buy a few good-quality pencils than have many cheaper ones that break easily and do not have rich colors.

4. Show by example. When showing our child how to use art materials, it is often better to draw squiggles or loose lines than draw a picture. If we show them a perfect-looking flower and they can only scribble, some children will not try at all.

And although it is fun and highly recommended to create together, side by side, it's better to take our own piece of paper than to draw on our child's paper. We do not know the child's intention for the work. Think of it as a fellow student's picture in an art class. Would we draw a little love heart on their self-portrait?

The best example of all is to hang beautiful artwork from artists on the walls of our home and at child height, too, for the whole family to appreciate.

05 / LANGUAGE

> "There is a 'sensitive period' for naming things . . . and if adults respond to the hunger for words in an appropriate way, they can give their children a richness and precision of language that will last a lifetime."
>
> —Dr. Silvana Montanaro, *Understanding the Human Being*

We have an amazing opportunity to expose our toddlers to beautiful, rich language that they will absorb with ease. Just as a child can learn the names of different fruits (bananas, apples, grapes, and so on), they can learn the names of different vehicles, from front-end loader to mobile crane, or different birds, from flamingo to toucan. Have fun with it. Likely we will discover limitations in our own vocabulary when we don't know the name of a specific bird, tree, or truck. Then we can look up the names with our child to find out.

Vocabulary baskets (also known as nomenclature materials)

To help toddlers grow their desire to learn words, we can put together vocabulary baskets for them to explore. These baskets have objects classified by theme: items from the kitchen; Australian animals; tools; or musical instruments. This makes it easy for our child to learn new words in a group of familiar objects.

- The first type of vocabulary basket contains **real objects** that the child can touch, feel, and explore as we name them, such as three to five fruits or vegetables.
- The next level is **replica objects**. Because we can't have real elephants in our classrooms or homes, we use replicas to present more vocabulary objects. Again the child can hold the object in their hand as we name it—a very tactile, hands-on approach to learning language.
- The child is then ready to learn that a 3D object is the same as a 2D picture. We can make **matching identical cards** with pictures of the objects on them so the child can match the object to a picture that is exactly the same. It's nice to take photos of the objects and print them so the image is the same size as the object—toddlers love to place the matching object on top to "hide" the picture underneath.
- Once a child is matching pictures that are exactly the same as the objects, they will start **matching similar cards**. We can make a card with a picture of a garbage truck that looks similar to it but isn't exactly the same. They then have to really abstract

(continued on page 48)

HOW TO WORK WITH LANGUAGE MATERIALS

GIVING A THREE-PERIOD LESSON

PERIOD ONE
name the objects

The primary objective of vocabulary baskets is for the toddler to learn the word for something. We name each object as we look at it, turn it around, feel it, and explore it. We give just the name of the object, for example, *giraffe*, instead of a full description of a giraffe with a long neck and so on.

PERIOD TWO
play games

We can play games to see which objects they can identify. "Can you find me the whisk?" They show us the whisk, and we say, "You found the whisk." And we mix them up.

When working with the cards, we can play several games:

- Lay the cards down one by one and have the child find the object that matches.
- Ask the child to choose an object, and one by one show them the cards until they spot the matching card.
- Fan the cards with the pictures hidden from them and ask them to pick a card; then they can look for the matching object.

If they choose the wrong object to go with the card, make a mental note of which object names they are mixing up. We do not correct them and say "no." I might say something like, "Ah, you wanted to put the violin on the cello." At a later time we can go back to period one and present the names again.

PERIOD THREE
testing

With children over 3 years old, when we know they have mastered the name of an object, we can ask, "What is this?" The child is delighted they know the answer and are very pleased with themselves as they name the object. When they are younger than 3 years old, we do not do the third period, because they are often preverbal or may make a mistake, which undermines their confidence. Wait until our child absolutely knows the names of the objects before doing this step.

the essence of a garbage truck, rather than simply matching the size, color, or shape. This step can often be done by matching pictures in books to objects in our home. Our child may pick up a toy cockatoo and run over to their bookshelf to show us a picture of a cockatoo in their favorite book.

- The final step for toddlers is **vocabulary cards**. We can offer cards with pictures of objects around a theme—vehicles, gardening tools—to help children learn names.

Books

We can choose lovely books to share with our children, and we can read aloud often. Children under 6 years old base their understanding of the world on what they see around them. Therefore, they love books that reflect things they know from their daily life: books about going shopping, visiting grandparents, getting dressed, city life, the seasons, and colors. One of the favorites from our classroom is *Sunshine* by Jan Ormerod, a book without words that tells the story of a little girl waking up and getting ready to leave the house.

Don't be surprised if children read a book about a witch and think that witches are real and scary. The Montessori philosophy is to wait until they are over 6 years old to introduce fantasy (especially scary fantasy), when they begin to understand the difference between reality and fantasy.

What to look for in books:

- **Realistic pictures**. This is what children see in their daily lives and can immediately and more easily relate to—rather than having a bear driving a car, look for pictures of people behind the wheel.
- **Beautiful images.** Children will absorb the beauty of the artwork in the book, so look for gorgeous illustrations.
- **Number of words.** For young toddlers we may have single words or simple sentences on a page. This will build to longer sentences on a page for older toddlers. Older toddlers also enjoy rhyming books. And don't forget poetry books.
- **Different types of pages.** Start with board books; move on to paper pages as the child learns how to handle books. Lift-the-flap books are also fun for toddlers and teach children to be careful as they open the flaps.
- **Books we enjoy.** Children pick up a love of reading from adults, so choose books you will want to read many times, knowing that a toddler will often shout, "Again! Again!"
- **Books that reflect diversity.** Find books that reflect families, races, nationalities, and belief systems that are different from our own.

We show children how to handle books, just as we would show them how to carry a glass. We can slow our movements to turn the page carefully and replace the book with care on the shelf when finished.

Occasionally we may want to have a book in our collection that is not based in reality. Then I would point it out in a fun way. "Do bears really go to the library? Noooo. How interesting. This is pretend. Let's take a look at what happens."

Conversations with our child

Describe the world around us

The adults in the environment are a child's primary source of language, so we can use any moment during our day to describe what we are doing. This could be anything from walking outside to getting dressed in the morning to cooking dinner. Use rich language, giving the proper words for the things we find, like the names of dogs, vegetables, food, vehicles, trees, and birds.

Self-expression

Even a young toddler can have a conversation. Conversations help children learn that what they say is important and encourage language development. We can stop what we are doing, look them in the eye, let them take as long as they need, and—hard as it is—try not to finish their sentences.

If our child says "ba-ba" for ball, we can show we have listened by including the real word in a sentence. For example, "Yes, you threw the ball into the garden."

We can ask simple questions to help them expand their story. Or if the child is preverbal and we are not sure what they want to tell us, we can ask them to show us.

Moments of silence

Don't forget to include moments of silence in the day. It is difficult to filter out background noise, and it's not ideal for language acquisition. In addition, we adults like to give our children feedback on everything they do. But it is also okay to remain silent sometimes and allow our child to evaluate for themselves what they have done.

Children understand more than baby talk and simple instructions. They want to be included in the communications of our daily life.

1
5
2
6
3
7
4
8

01 / EYE-HAND COORDINATION

N°1 **PEG PUZZLE**
This peg puzzle has five pieces, which is perfect for a young toddler. The size of the knob is small to help refine their grasp. From around 18 months.

N°2 **POSTING**
The child works on refining their posting skills to fit a coin through a small slot. This is one of the favorite activities in our class for children starting around 16 months.

N°3 **NUTS AND BOLTS**
This set is great for organizing the nuts and bolts from smallest to largest and practicing putting the nut on the bolt. The child begins with placing the bolts in the correct holes. Older toddlers will love to master the nuts. From around 2 years.

N°4 **MYSTERY BAGS**
These mystery bags are for learning what an object is, using only the sense of touch. We can hide objects around a theme, paired objects, or—most difficult—random objects from around the home. From 2.5 years.

N°5 **THREADING**
Threading activities are great for the child to practice working with two hands together. We can vary the size of the beads and the thickness of the thread, depending on their ability. From 16 months.

N°6 **OPENING AND CLOSING**
Children love to find small objects inside old purses, jars with lids, or containers with different openings such as zippers, press studs, and clasps. From 18 months.

N°7 **SORTING**
Sorting by type, size, and color is interesting to toddlers. Sorting small buttons by color is for children from 2 years.

N°8 **PEGBOARD AND ELASTICS**
I love watching toddlers develop their eye-hand coordination with this activity. They learn to stretch elastic bands over the pegs, which takes great concentration. Older children also use this activity to make some fun patterns. From around 2 years.

1
2
3
4
SWAN
HARMONICA
5
EARLY RIDER
6
7
8

02 / MUSIC AND MOVEMENT

N°1 **STRIKING**
Making sounds by striking/banging an instrument is perfect for both young and older toddlers. Think of triangles, drums, tone blocks, and xylophones. With a younger toddler, assist if needed (for example, hold the triangle while they strike it). For any age toddler.

N°2 **SHAKING**
Instruments that make sound by shaking are the easiest instruments to begin with. I love the variety of maracas available, from egg shaped to the more traditional kind. Look out for rainmakers, which make soothing sounds as the beads fall or are shaken. For any age toddler.

N°3 **MUSIC BOX**
Turning a handle to make music is enjoyable for toddlers. Younger toddlers may need some assistance at first, perhaps with the adult holding the music box while they turn it. Seek out large, solid versions for younger toddlers. Older toddlers will enjoy the challenge of turning a smaller music maker (as pictured on opposite page). For any age toddler.

N°4 **BLOWING**
Simple instruments like a harmonica or recorder are fun for toddlers. They can experiment with rhythm, speed, and volume, and perhaps a variety of notes. For an older toddler.

N°5 **BALANCE BIKE**
Once the child is tall enough, a balance bike without pedals can be a great alternative to a traditional tricycle. Riding on two wheels, they push themselves along with their feet. Then gradually they begin to take their feet off the ground while they coast, getting used to the feeling of balancing—a useful step before they learn to ride a bike. With time and at their own pace, they often transition easily to a regular bike without training wheels. From around 2 years.

N°6 **OUTSIDE**
Heading out into nature, making nature collections, and crafting with treasures from our walks are just a few of the ways to enjoy the outside with young children. Go outside often—just add some weatherproof clothing if needed! For any age toddler.

N°7 **BALLS**
Taking a variety of balls outside encourages kicking, rolling, coordination, strength, and, of course, fun. For toddlers, it is generally best to use balls outside, so that they have enough space to play. For any age toddler.

N°8 **SLIDE**
This is a Pikler slide, which could be used inside the home. The height of the slide can be adjusted as the child grows. They can also enjoy climbing up the slide as much as sliding down. Or look for a slide on a playground, preferably one they can manage independently. For any age toddler.

1
2
3
4
5
6
7

03 / PRACTICAL LIFE

N°1 CARE OF SELF

There are many opportunities for our child to learn how to look after themselves as we gradually scaffold their skills so they can do more and more for themselves. They love to master these tasks, including brushing their hair and their teeth, blowing their nose, and washing their hands. From 15 months.

N°2 FOOD PREPARATION

Toddlers love to make their own snack or help with meal preparation. Look for tools that are suited to small hands so they can succeed. At first the child will need some assistance. For example, first we can show them how to peel the apple. Then we can hold the apple on a board while they peel from top to bottom, putting the peel into a bowl to take to the compost bin afterward. We show them how to place their hands safely on the apple cutter. We can slice the apple across the middle so the child can easily push the apple cutter through the fruit. Apple cutting from 2 years.

N°3 TABLE SETTING

Use a low cupboard to provide toddlers access to their bowl, cutlery, and glass so they can set the table following a marked place mat as a guide.

N°4 BAKING

Toddlers can help to add ingredients that we have measured, mix ingredients with a wooden spoon, knead dough, use cookie cutters, and decorate baked goods. And yes, they also can help us with tasting the finished product. From 12 months.

N°5 WINDOW CLEANING

It is amazing how toddlers are able to manage squeezing a spray bottle to clean the windows—the repeated movement is great for their hand strength. Then they can wipe the windows from top to bottom with a squeegee and use a cloth to dry them. We can use water or add some vinegar to make the windows sparkle. From 18 months.

N°6 FLOWER ARRANGING

Flower arranging is a multistep process that allows the toddler to refine their fine-motor skills and practice carrying and pouring water with control—all while adding beauty to the home. First, they can fill a very small jug with water from the tap and place it on a tray to catch any water that might spill. Using a small funnel, they can pour the water into the vase. Then they can place a flower in the vase and place the vase on a doily (which is a nice extra step, good for developing concentration). Have a sponge at the ready for small spills. From 18 months.

N°7 CLEANING

Having small cleaning tools at the ready—for example, a broom, a mop, a dustpan and brush, hand mitts, and sponges—allows the toddler to learn to care for the home. Most toddlers love to help sweep, mop, and dust. This small dustpan and brush are useful for sweeping up crumbs and provide great practice for working with two hands together. From 12 months.

1
2
3
4
5
STABILO

6
7

04 / ARTS AND CRAFTS

N°1 **WATERCOLOR PAINTING**
Watercolors are perfect for toddlers who want to paint—even a young toddler can have success, without as much potential for mess as markers or paint. Start with just one color. Look for single watercolor tablets, pop out one color from a watercolor palette, or cut the palette into single colors if possible. The child can practice wetting the brush, getting paint onto the brush, and making marks on the paper. They are not learning how to draw at this age—they are learning how to use the materials and how to express their movements on paper. From 18 months.

N°2 **SEWING**
Start with a simple sewing card, a blunt darning needle, and thread that is doubled and knotted at the end. We can show them how to push the needle into the hole, turn the card over, and pull the needle out the other side. Then the needle goes into the next hole, the card is turned over, and again the needle is pulled through, making a stitch. When the card is complete, cut the thread with scissors to remove the needle and make a knot. From 2 years.

N°3 **SCISSORS**
First the child learns how to hold the scissors safely while sitting at the table. At first, they use two hands to open and close the scissors. Then we can introduce cutting, starting with a sturdy piece of card cut into thin strips. Hold the strip for them to snip. The pieces can be collected into a bowl and then placed into a small envelope and sealed with a sticker. Repeat. As their hand strength develops, they will be able to hold the scissors in one hand and hold the strip for themselves. Around 2 years.

N°4 **SCRIBBLING**
My favorite scribbling materials for toddlers are soft chunky pencils and beeswax crayon blocks. We can change the paper size, color, and material from time to time to offer variety. Again, they are learning how to use the materials rather than learning to draw. From 12 months.

N°5 **CHALK AND ERASER**
Offer chunky chalk that fits easily in the child's hands, and provide a large surface, such as a big chalkboard or the sidewalk. A large surface allows movement of the whole arm as they practice using the chalk and cleaning with the eraser. From 12 months.

N°6 **GLUING**
Affixing small shapes onto paper with a glue brush and a small pot of glue helps refine movements. (Alternatively, offer a glue stick.) The glue can be brushed onto the back of the shape, then turned over and stuck onto the paper. From 18 months.

N°7 **CLAY/PLAY DOUGH/KINETIC SAND**
Working clay with their hands and using simple tools encourages the child's hand strength and creativity. The clay can be rolled flat, made into a log, cut into small pieces, rolled into a ball, or molded in infinite ways. I love to switch out the clay for play dough or kinetic sand from time to time to provide a variety of sensorial experiences. From 16 months.

1
2
Sunshine
Jan Ormerod
Planting a Rainbow by Lois Ehlert
4
3

5

05 / LANGUAGE

N°1 **REPLICA OBJECTS**
To learn new vocabulary, we can offer realistic replicas around a theme like cooking implements, African animals, or musical instruments. The child can touch and feel around the object while they hear its name—another example of learning with concrete materials. For any age toddler.

N°2 **CARDS**
As the child gets older, we can extend opportunities to build vocabulary by offering cards with pictures around a theme. That way we are not limited by the replicas or objects we can find. Featured here are artworks by Vincent van Gogh. From 18 months.

N°3 **BOOKS**
Reading with our toddlers is a joy when we find books we both love. Look for books about seasons, daily life, animals, colors, shapes, vehicles, nature, and our child's favorite topics. For older toddlers, we can add books filled with details to explore or counting books. For any age toddler.

N°4 **REAL OBJECTS**
The most direct way for the child to learn vocabulary is from objects in their daily life. Just as they learn the names of fruit, we can name flowers in our home and at the market, trees and birds we see in the park, and items around the house. Shown here are some garden peas and a set of cards, where the child learns that a three-dimensional object can be represented by a two-dimensional image. From 12 months. With cards from 14 months.

N°5 **OBJECTS WITH CARDS (IDENTICAL AND SIMILAR)**
We can draw or photograph an object to make a set of identical cards. Once the child is able to match objects with cards that are identical, we can increase the difficulty by using images that are similar to the objects but not exactly the same. The object may be a dump truck, and we would offer them a picture of any dump truck (of a different model, color, size). This helps them understand the essence of a dump truck. With cards from 14 months.

AN EXTRA NOTE ON THE OUTDOORS AND NATURE

> "Let the children be free; encourage them; let them run outside when it is raining; let them remove their shoes when they find a puddle of water; and, when the grass of the meadows is damp with dew, let them run on it and trample it with their bare feet; let them rest peacefully when a tree invites them to sleep beneath its shade; let them shout and laugh when the sun wakes them in the morning as it wakes every living creature that divides its day between waking and sleeping."
>
> —Dr. Maria Montessori, *The Discovery of the Child*

I love how even in the early 1900s, Dr. Montessori had such a holistic idea of children and their development, including the importance of the outdoors and nature. Nature has the ability to calm us, to connect us with beauty, and to reconnect us to the earth and environment.

Young children are sensorial learners. The quote from Dr. Montessori above embodies how rich their experiences can be. Even now as an adult, the memories of walking barefoot in the grass from my own childhood are still so strong.

If we live in the city, we can plan adventures in nature every few months. It might be for an afternoon at the seaside or spending a few nights away in a tent or cabin.

Here are some ways to include Montessori activities outdoors and in nature:

1. **Seasonal activities.** Depending on the season we could take a basket to the local park or a nearby forest to collect leaves, acorns, shells, sticks, rocks, stones, and pinecones. Fruit picking varies by season, too.

2. **Grow vegetables.** It isn't necessary to have a garden to grow vegetables at home. Set up a potting station with some soil, a scoop, and some seeds. Have a watering can at the ready. Composting—adding food waste to a compost bin or worm farm—helps our children learn about the food cycle and returning nutrients to the soil.

3. **Movement opportunities.** Climb trees; balance along walls, tree stumps, or logs; hang from branches; swing from a tire; ride a balance bike; kick a ball; jump with a jump rope; chase each other; run fast; and walk slowly.

4. **Notice the beauty of the outdoors together.** Watch insects at work, droplets on leaves, the colors of the sunset, the vistas from the mountains, the stillness or the ripples on a lake, the movement of the ocean, or the wind in the trees, or simply take in the gloriousness of the flowers and bees in a neighbor's garden. Grab a magnifying glass to explore close up, touch with our hands, listen to the movement of the trees and grass, and smell the rain or flowers.

5. **Find moments of quiet.** Find a place to sit and watch the clouds, to sit in silence, or just to breathe.

6. **Make treasure hunts.** Make a list of pictures and work together to find all the items on the list. It could be in the garden, at the park, in the forest, or any outdoor place.

7. **Build a hut, cubby house, or obstacle course, and invite over some friends.**

8. **Make outdoor art.** Use mud, water, leaves, flowers, soil, seeds, grass, and any other natural treasures that you find. Lay them into patterns, make them into shapes, or work together to make a face or an animal.

9. **Make a musical wall.** In the garden, hang old pots and pans, bells, and any other objects that make some sound when banged. Find some sticks to make some music.

10. **All-weather exploration.** There is no such thing as bad weather, just bad clothing. So get some great all-weather clothing and shoes (for the adult and the child) and stomp in those puddles, make a snowman, or put on a hat and sunscreen and explore the beach. Get out each and every day.

Bonus: **Anything to do with water**—spraying the windows, filling a bucket and painting bricks with a brush, running through a sprinkler, making rivers with sand and water, or using a water pump at the playground.

WHAT ABOUT NON-MONTESSORI TOYS?

There is a difference between a Montessori classroom and a Montessori home. Although we would not include these toys in a Montessori classroom, we may choose to include a few well-selected toys for open-ended play at home. If we are new to the Montessori approach, we can start with the toys we already have in our homes—keep out our child's favorites, donate the ones that are no longer being used, and put some toys into storage that we will rotate later.

Here are some ideas:

- Duplo/Lego
- wooden blocks
- construction vehicles, emergency vehicles, farm vehicles
- barn and farm animals
- Playmobil sets based on daily life (rather than fantasy, like princesses or pirates)
- a wooden marble run
- loose parts collected from nature adventures
- construction sets
- train sets
- board games

There is room for such open-ended play in the home—the child explores the materials in many creative ways, makes discoveries for themselves, and plays out imaginative scenarios from their daily lives. Yet they aren't a replacement for the Montessori activities we have discussed in this chapter, which give a toddler such satisfaction from mastery and meet so many of a young child's developmental needs.

If a child starts attending a Montessori preschool program, I'd advise against replicating the Montessori materials at home so that they will stay engaged at school. Instead we can continue Montessori at home by including the child in daily life and making sure they have time for unstructured play, opportunities to create, time outdoors, and time for rest. They will continue to practice skills through practical life, arts and crafts, movement and music, and books.

TO PRACTICE

1. Can we provide eye-hand coordination activities to challenge our child's fine-motor skills?
2. Can we provide rich music and movement opportunities?
3. Can we include our child in daily life (practical life activities)?
   food preparation / self-care / care of the environment
4. What arts and crafts possibilities are available?
5. How can we support a rich language environment at home?
   objects / books / conversation

In this chapter, we have seen how observing our children's interests and abilities and providing them with beautiful and engaging activities can help develop the whole child.

We can use items we already have in the home, and Montessori activities don't need to be fully integrated from the first day. Instead we can try a few things to shift toward a Montessori approach at home, observe our child more, build our own confidence, and keep following the child.

And, let's not forget the simplest things, the things that will create memories with our children:

- Let's savor the laughter and giggles.
- Let's invite our children to share in the daily activities of the home.
- Let's enjoy the puddles when it rains.
- Let's collect autumn leaves and hang them in the window.
- Let's build tents indoors.
- Let's leave our children to explore a moment longer.
- Let's comb the beach for shells, in any season.
- Let's cuddle our loved ones an extra time or two.
- Let's enjoy the crispness of the air as we cycle through the city.

SETTING UP THE HOME

4

SETTING UP MONTESSORI-STYLE SPACES

Walk into a Montessori classroom for the first time, and it is immediately apparent that the space has been beautifully arranged with the children's needs in mind.

The same principles are easy to apply in the home. We aren't aiming to have a perfect home, but we can be intentional in setting up our spaces.

Not every space has to be child-sized. After all, there are different-sized people with different needs in our home. However, it is possible to have a space in each area of our home that is set up for our child to enjoy and feel comfortable in, too.

Eight tips for setting up your home

1. **Child-sized.** Find furniture that the child can manage without help. Look for chairs and tables that are the right height to allow their feet to sit flat on the floor; cut the legs of the furniture a bit if necessary.
2. **Beauty in the space.** Display art and plants at the child's height for them to enjoy.
3. **Independence.** Have activities and materials set up in trays and baskets so they have everything they need at the ready; look for ways to make it easy for the child to help themselves.
4. **Attractive activities.** Have age-appropriate activities beautifully arranged on shelves—rather than in toy boxes—that are inviting to them.
5. **Less is more.** Displaying only a few activities helps the child's concentration; display only the ones they are working to master, so they don't feel overwhelmed.
6. **A place for everything and everything in its place.** Toddlers have a particularly strong sense of order. When we have a place for everything and everything is in its place, it helps them learn where things belong (and where to put them away).
7. **See the space through their eyes.** Get down to the child's height in each space to see what it looks like from their perspective. We may see some tempting wires or some clutter under the shelves, or it may feel overwhelming.
8. **Store and rotate.** Create storage that ideally is out of children's sight and easy on the eye—think floor-to-ceiling cupboards that blend into the wall color, an attic space, or containers that can be stacked in a storage area or behind a couch. Store most of the child's activities, and rotate the activities on their shelves when they are looking for new challenges.

ROOM BY ROOM

Let's look at the different areas of our home and see how these principles can be applied. (For a resource list, see page 226.)

These are only ideas and are not prescriptive. Adapt them to suit. Limitations of space or light give us opportunities to be creative.

Entrance

- Low hooks at the child's height where they can hang up their (child-sized) backpack/bag, jacket, hat, and raincoat
- Basket or shelf for shoes
- Basket for seasonal items such as mittens, scarves, woolen hats, sunglasses, and so on
- Low mirror with a small table or shelf for things like tissues, hair clips, and sunscreen
- Low chair or bench where they can sit to put on their shoes and take them off

Note: If we have more than one child, we may choose to have one basket per child.

Living room

- Low two- or three-tier shelves for activities. If we have more than one child, we can use lower shelves for the younger child's activities and higher shelves for older children's activities. Be sure the higher shelves are out of reach of the younger sibling, or use containers that the younger child cannot manage to open. For reference, the shelves in my classroom are 40" long by 12" deep by 15" high (120 cm by 30 cm by 40 cm).
- Small table and chair, preferably by a window—cut the legs down if needed so the child can put their feet flat on the floor. For example, the chair seat height would be around 8 inches (20 cm) and the table height around 14 inches (35 cm).
- Easy-to-roll floor mats (around 27 inches by 20 inches, or 70 cm by 50 cm) stored in a basket and used to mark a space for their activity.

Kitchen

- Low shelf, cupboard, trolley, or drawer with a small number of child-sized plates, cutlery, glasses, and place mats
  - Use real glasses, plates, and cutlery—children will learn to carry these items with care if they are aware that the items may break. We can remind them that glass is fragile and to use two hands (rather than saying, "Don't drop the glass").
- Stepladder or learning tower or kitchen helper so the child can reach the kitchen counter to help (alternatively, bring food preparation items to the dining table or a low table)
- Child-sized cleaning materials
  - broom, mop, small dustpan, and brush
  - hand mitts (cloths where the hand fits inside; easy for a child to use to wipe up spills)
  - sponges cut to fit their hands
  - dust cloth
  - child-sized aprons
- Child-sized kitchen implements for food preparation
  - apple cutter and corer
  - metal juicer with arm to pull down, orange squeezer or electric juicer to squeeze orange juice
  - little spreaders that toddlers can use easily to spread their favorite topping onto small crackers (stored in a container)
- Cutting implements
  - start with nonserrated butter knives for cutting soft items such as bananas
  - offer a crinkle cutter for firmer fruits and vegetables
  - increase difficulty as the child's skills build, for example, sharper knives may be introduced with a cutting guide as they become preschoolers (with supervision)
- Water source so the child can help themselves to a drink—a water dispenser that they can reach, a low sink, or a little water in a small jug on a tray (with a sponge or cloth at the ready for spills)
- Easy-to-open containers with nutritious snacks—put out only as much food as we are happy for them to eat between meals. If they choose to eat it right after breakfast, the snacks are done for the day.
- Measuring cups and spoons, a scale, and mixing spoons for baking
- Spray bottle and squeegee for cleaning windows
- Small watering can, if there are indoor plants

Note about safety: Keep sharp knives out of reach and show the child how to use them when they are ready; be available to supervise.

Eating area

- For snack time, children could use their low table and chair, and encourage them to keep food at the table (don't let them walk around with food).
- At mealtimes, I like to sit together as a family at the kitchen/dining table. Look for a chair the child is able to climb in and out of independently, like a Stokke chair or one similar to it.
- Have a child-sized jug on the table at mealtimes with a small amount of water or milk so children can help themselves—fill with only as much as we are prepared to clean up.
- Have hand mitts or sponges at the ready for spills.
- A small basket can be used to carry items from the kitchen to set the table. If we are setting the dining table for the meal, we may need a stepstool for our child to be able to reach the table.
- A place mat with a guide where to place the plate, cutlery, and glass can be useful for a toddler. One of the parents in my classes had the great idea to photograph her child's favorite set, print it on letter-sized paper, and laminate it—a perfect guide for the child to use when setting the table.
- Some (handpicked) flowers on the table make mealtimes a special occasion every day.

Bedroom

- Floor mattress or toddler bed that the child can climb in and out of by themselves
- If space allows, a small shelf with a few activities for them to quietly play with when they wake
- Book basket or shelf
- Full-length mirror—helps the child see their full body schema, and aids dressing
- A small wardrobe with shelves, drawers, or hanging space that the child can reach. Or use a basket with limited choices of seasonally appropriate clothing to choose from each day. Store out-of-season clothing out of reach to avoid potential battles.
- Ensure the room is completely childproof—cover electrical sockets, remove any loose wires, put curtain cords (which present a choking hazard) out of reach, and install child locks on windows.

Bathroom

- A changing area. Once they are standing, children wearing diapers often don't like to be laid down to be changed. Instead, we can change them standing up in the bathroom to introduce them to the idea that this is where they will use the toilet. We can also start to offer the potty or toilet as part of the changing routine (more on toileting in chapter 7).
- Low step to help them to reach the bathroom sink and to climb into the bath
- Small bar of soap or a soap pump they can manage by themselves to wash hands
- Toothbrush, toothpaste, hairbrush within the child's reach
- Mirror at the child's height or accessible to them
- Basket for dirty/wet clothing (or in the laundry area)
- Low hook or towel rack for the child to have access to their towel
- Small travel-sized bottles for body wash, shampoo, and conditioner that the child can learn to use. Refill them each day with a small amount if they like to squeeze bottles.

Arts and crafts area

- Access to art materials—for example, a small set of drawers with pencils, paper, glue, stamps, and collage items
- As the child gets older, we can include access to scissors, tape, and a stapler.
- Choose fewer but higher-quality art materials.
- For toddlers, activities can be set out on trays with everything at the ready—for example, one tray for drawing and one tray for gluing.
- Around 3 years, the child will start to enjoy collecting things they will need. Then we may have a tray they can use to select art materials by themselves from a display.
- Make putting things away easy: a place for artwork to dry; a place for scraps of paper that can be reused; a place for recycling.
- Toddlers are mostly interested in the process, not the product, so here are some ideas for finished artwork:
  - Use office "in-trays" for things they want to keep or come back to; once the trays are full, glue a selection of favorites in a scrapbook.
  - Keep a record of artwork that is too bulky to keep by photographing it.
  - Reuse the artwork as gift paper.
  - Encourage children to work on both sides of the paper.
  - Make a gallery to feature some of the child's artwork. For example, have frames where the work is rotated, a string or wire where work is hung up, or magnets on the fridge.

Cozy place for reading

- Have a forward-facing bookshelf or ledge so the child can easily see the cover of the books. Or use a book basket.
- Display only a few books and change the selection as needed.
- Provide a beanbag, cushions, low chair, or cozy floor mat.
- Near the window gives lovely light to read by.
- Make a cozy space in an old wardrobe by removing the wardrobe doors, or have a pup tent to crawl into.

Outside

- Create opportunities for movement activities: running; jumping; skipping; hopping; brachiating (swinging like a monkey); sliding; dancing; swinging on a rope, an old tire, or a regular swing
- Gardening—small rakes, trowels, garden forks, wheelbarrow
- A small vegetable garden they can help care for. If we are able to grow vegetables in a raised garden bed, in pots on a balcony, or inside, they will also learn to appreciate their food by seeing where it comes from and how long it takes to grow and nurture.
- A place to sit or lie quietly to watch the clouds
- Water—a bucket of water and a paintbrush to "paint" the bricks or concrete pavers, spray bottles to wash windows, a water table, a water pump
- Sand pit
- Labyrinth with small rocks to make a path
- Place by the door where they can put on outside shoes or brush off their shoes to come inside
- Baskets and jars for making (seasonal) nature collections
- Digging in dirt, making mud, reconnecting with the earth
- Huts or tunnels made from willow branches
- Create secret paths for the child to explore

There are many sources of inspiration for our outside spaces. I love seeing "natural playscapes" where natural elements are incorporated into the design. For example, a slide built into a slope in the yard, or paths made from natural rocks or found materials. For inspiration, look up Rusty Keeler, who creates such natural playscapes for children.

Note: If there is no outside space at home, look to provide such possibilities at a nearby playground, woods, beach, lake, or mountains.

AT-HOME STARTER SET FOR MONTESSORI TODDLERS

Here are eight basic pieces of equipment to introduce Montessori at home at very little expense.

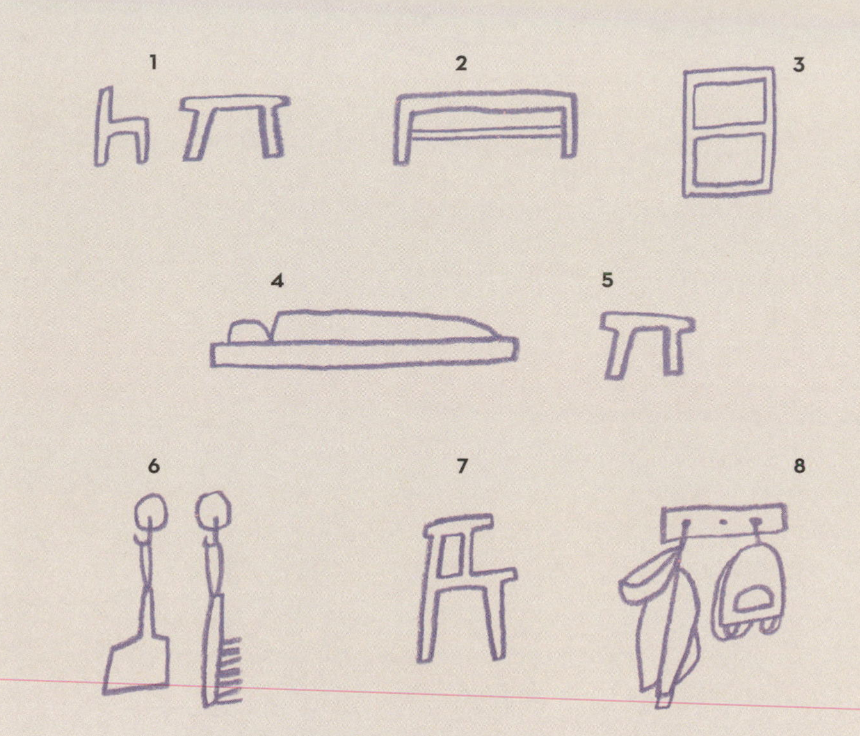

1. small table and chair **2.** low shelf **3.** bookshelf/book box **4.** low bed/floor mattress child can get into themselves **5.** low stool for reaching sink, toilet, and so on **6.** low hooks with cleaning equipment **7.** stepladder/learning tower for helping in the kitchen **8.** low hooks for coat and bag by the entrance

GENERAL PRINCIPLES TO KEEP IN MIND

Tackling the clutter

Some may be thinking, *I could never keep such a tidy house. We have too many things.*

The first step is to reduce the number of toys, books, and arts and crafts materials, and the general mess that accumulates in our homes. Place into a box the activities and toys our child is not using very often or things they are finding too difficult. This box can be stored for now; we can rotate and reintroduce these activities when our child needs a new challenge. Place into a second box items that are for younger children, activities that they do not use anymore or are too easy. Find a new home for them or keep them aside for a younger sibling.

Keep out just the few things the child is using a lot. It's about continually finding the right number of activities to keep the toddler engaged without holding on to ones that no longer capture their interest.

This will be an ongoing process that will eventually include our child, developing ideas about reusing, recycling, charity, and taking care of our toys with the idea that they can be passed along when we are ready for something new.

Toddlers do not let go of items easily. Get them used to the idea that the items are going into a box for charity or for another family. Offer them one last turn to play with an item; they can put it into the box when they are all finished. They can then help you carry it out of the house to deliver it. And if the box can't be delivered straight away, remove it from view so the child doesn't have to repeat the parting process.

For those interested in adopting an even more minimalist approach at home, I recommend looking up Marie Kondo, the author of *The Life-Changing Magic of Tidying Up*. She recommends keeping only those things in our homes that bring us joy or are useful. Imagine applying the same principle to our child's activities and clothing. And always saying "thank you" to the things we no longer need or use before letting them go.

Making it cozy

Getting rid of clutter does not mean that our home should be without character. We can place cushions, blankets, plants, and artwork at the child's height. Choose natural materials for baskets and carpets to add warmth.

Our homes are adapted to the country and time we live in. With varied family origins, we may display treasures or furniture from these other cultures, in addition to incorporating their rituals and traditions.

I love adding handmade elements like paper bunting, hand-knitted or hand-sewn items, or other crafts that we have created together. These details make a home distinctive and special, something that our child will absorb and cherish.

Vintage items can also make a home unique and full of personality without feeling overly cluttered.

All these elements make a house a home, with the goal of making the space feel calm, warm, and accessible to our child.

Setting up our home to save us work

Raising toddlers can be a lot of work, and we can get pretty tired. So we can also set up our homes to make things easier for them and, consequently, for ourselves.

Arrange things so children can manage more independently and successfully. Have things they need at their height, so that they're easily accessible. Remove items that are not suitable for them to touch. Keep adjusting and improving, particularly as the child grows.

Susan Stephenson, an experienced Montessori teacher, shared this story with me. She would note each time a child asked for help in her class and then set up a way the child would be able to help themselves the next time. So if the child asked for a tissue, a tissue box could be placed at the child's height; if they pulled out all the tissues, a small basket could hold a few tissues carefully folded, ready for use.

Remember, we want our homes to be "yes" spaces that are safe for our toddlers to explore. When we find ourselves saying "no"—for example, when our child is touching something dangerous or banging on glass—we can look for ways to set up the space to remove the temptation. We can cover an electrical outlet that is proving tempting, move furniture to block places we don't want them to explore, use child safety locks on a cupboard we don't want opened, or put a fragile glass cabinet into storage until our child is a little older.

If we can't make the whole home safe, we can at least make one area a "yes" space where our child can play freely, perhaps with a baby gate across the door. (We still want them to be able to move a lot, so avoid playpens, which will limit their movement.)

Sharing spaces

If we have more than one child, here are some extra things to consider:

- Set up spaces for different ages
  - Use lower shelves for activities for the younger child or for any age; use higher shelves for activities with smaller parts more suitable for the older children.
  - Store small parts in containers that are difficult for younger children to open.
  - Establish a place or two where each child can go to be by themselves. This can be as simple as making a hiding place with two chairs and a blanket. We can even hang a sign on the outside that says "Private" and point to it when their sibling comes close. We can tell them, "It says private. It looks like they want to be alone right now. Let's find something else to do."
  - If a younger sibling is interfering, try to simplify the activity so they are able to participate.
- Sharing toys
  - Come up with a plan for how toys and activities will be shared. (See chapter 7 for more information on sharing.)
- Sharing a room
  - Personalize each child's area with, for example, a shelf above their bed with personal items, photos, and collections.
  - Provide privacy if needed, perhaps using a curtain to divide the room.
  - Make clear agreements about using the space, like when to turn the lights off.
  - Set up the space so each child can be alone somewhere.

Small spaces

It's easy to think that it would be easier to apply these principles if we had a larger home. However, it is possible—and perhaps even essential—to use these ideas if our home is smaller. We want to make the best use of the limited space available, which otherwise becomes easily cluttered and overwhelming. I see limitations like small spaces as opportunities for creativity.

Here are some ideas to help:

- Use bunk beds/high beds, or store beds away during the day using Japanese-style futon mattresses.
- Buy multifunctional furniture or get rid of some furniture to create space to play.
- Look for light-framed, less bulky furniture and use a neutral palette to give a feeling of more space.
- Keep fewer things on display at a time to keep the space from feeling cluttered.
- Use space on the walls (such as pegboards to hang craft materials) or underused spaces for storage (under beds, for example), or disguise cabinets for storage near the ceiling (perhaps by painting them the same color as the wall).

THE IMPORTANCE OF THE HOME ENVIRONMENT

These ideas should help inspire us to reduce the chaos and create more engaging spaces for our child.

Other benefits include:

- Encouraging the child to take part in daily life
- Aiding their independence
- Providing peaceful, nurturing, and creative spaces for the whole family
- Helping build the child's concentration with less clutter and fewer, more focused activities
- Allowing the child to absorb and appreciate beauty
- Beginning to show them how to be responsible for their things
- Helping them absorb the culture(s) in which they live

Setting up our home can help to create some calm in our life with our child. I hope these ideas serve as inspiration to make a few changes today. We can always continue to work on our homes, gradually making things even more accessible, more attractive, and more engaging for our child.

TO PRACTICE

1. Can we provide
   - child-sized furniture?
   - beauty, for example, with plants and art?
   - ways for our child to be independent?
   - attractive activities?
   - less clutter?
   - a place for everything and everything in its place?
   - storage?
2. Can we see the space through our child's eyes?
3. Can we make a space in each room of our home for our child?

HOME TOUR

Austria

Now it's time to be inspired by the home of Anna, from Eltern vom Mars.

Let's take a look at Anna's Montessori home in Austria. Everything is set out at the child's height, and the space is simple and beautiful. The child has everything in its place and at the ready. The simple color palette is so calming. Can we please move in?

SELF-CARE AREA

This small self-care area is simple and attractive. Here the child can blow their nose, wipe their face, or brush their hair. A low stool holds two baskets, one with tissues and the other with a hairbrush. A small basket underneath is for dirty tissues. The mirror hung vertically allows the child to see their full body and is perfect for a quick check as they leave the house.

ARTS AND CRAFTS AREA

This arts and crafts area is set up for an older toddler. The open shelves are inviting and accessible, and the use of trays and containers makes it easy to see what is available.

The pencils on the top shelf look attractive, set up by color in simple DIY glass jars with a sticker for each color.

Small pots contain beads and thread for threading activities; materials like washi tape, a hole punch, and scissors are at the ready; marker pens are displayed in a see-through container; and paintbrushes and watercolor are also available.

A plant softens the space, and a music player is available for the child to independently select music.

A small table and chair are next to this shelf where the child can use these materials (not pictured).

KITCHEN

A low drawer in the kitchen allows the child to help themselves to food preparation tools.

Cutlery is held in jars, and baskets hold a rolling pin, whisk, and peeler. Also available are a small grater, juicer, egg slicer, and apple cutter/corer.

OUTSIDE

A paved area has been transformed into a beautiful outdoor space to explore.

We can see a broom and gardening tools hung on hooks at the ready, alongside a watering can and bucket. Potted plants are fun to water, and vertical space has been used for more plants.

When the weather allows, this area is also used for working with other activities, simply using a small breakfast tray or sitting at a table and chair.

RAISING A CURIOUS CHILD

WHO FEELS SEEN AND HEARD

5

PART ONE

ENCOURAGING CURIOSITY IN OUR CHILD

PART TWO

ACCEPTING OUR CHILD FOR WHO THEY ARE

PART ONE

ENCOURAGING CURIOSITY IN OUR CHILD

As we discussed in chapter 2, Montessori teachers do not believe a child is a vessel to be filled with facts. The child genuinely loves learning, making discoveries for themselves, and coming up with creative solutions.

As parents we can also encourage curiosity in our children at home with five ingredients.

FIVE INGREDIENTS FOR CURIOSITY

1. Trust in the child

Dr. Montessori encourages us to trust that the child wants to learn and grow—and that the child intrinsically knows what they need to be working on to develop as they should. This means that if we provide them with a rich environment to explore, we don't need to force them to learn or be worried if they are developing "differently" from their peers.

We can trust that they are developing along their unique path, in their unique way, on their unique timeline.

We can also trust them to learn the limits of their bodies for themselves. Toddlers are curious learners who want to explore the world around them. There may be accidents along the way that we cannot prevent (and maybe that we should allow to happen). After all, that is how they learn. And we will be there if they want to be held. "Ow. Was that a shock? It's hard to see you hurt yourself. I'm so glad your body is made to heal itself. Isn't it amazing?"

Are we constantly worrying about how our child is developing or whether they will hurt themselves? Can we practice setting aside those worries about the future and enjoy where they are today, on their unique journey?

2. A rich learning environment

For a child to develop curiosity in the world around them and a desire to learn, we must provide a rich learning environment and time to explore it.

This rich learning environment does not have to be filled with expensive materials. Explorations in nature can be totally free, dropping a chain or string into a cardboard tube can cost nothing, and sorting out some dried beans can cost very little.

What we learned in chapter 3 about activities was to keep observing our child and offer them opportunities to practice what they are mastering right now.

What does our child's environment look like—the physical, the social, even the adults around them? Does it provide them with rich opportunities for exploration?

3. Time

For children to develop and follow their urge to discover, explore, and wonder, they need time. Time that is unscheduled. Time that is not rushed. Even times when they feel bored.

Allow time to explore. Allow time for movement. Allow time for language and conversation. Allow time for building connections. Allow time for wonder and curiosity.

Whether we work or are with our child full-time, let's think creatively about our days and weeks. Can we change things to carve out 15 to 30 minutes of unscheduled time every day? Perhaps an hour or two on the weekend? What commitments can we let go of?

4. A safe and secure base

As a parent we can provide physical and emotional safety and security. We keep our child physically safe from electrical outlets, busy roads, and other dangers. We childproof our homes, or at least one area of it, so that our child can freely explore.

Emotionally we can give them safety, too. We can accept them for who they are. And they can trust us to be there for them even when they are having a hard time.

This safety and sense of security allow the child the freedom to be curious in the world.

Are there ways to show our child that we are there for them, even (and particularly) when they are having a hard time? Are we able to look them in the eye and acknowledge the big feelings they are having about things that seem small to us?

5. Fostering a sense of wonder

We can ask our child questions about the world we see, invite them to explore with all their senses, and get out into nature as often as possible.

Are we modeling wonder for our child? Do we allow them to explore with all their senses? Do we use nature to inspire a sense of wonder in our child?

SEVEN PRINCIPLES FOR CURIOUS HUMANS

When we ensure these five ingredients are available to our child, they have a strong base from which to become curious about the world around them and develop the ability to think and do things for themselves.

With a foundation of the five basic ingredients, we can apply seven principles to help them become curious human beings.

1. Follow the child—let them lead.
2. Encourage hands-on learning—let them explore.
3. Include the child in daily life—let them be included.
4. Go slow—let them set their own pace.
5. Help me to help myself—let them be independent and responsible.
6. Encourage creativity—let them wonder.
7. Observe—let them show us.

Let's take each one in turn to explore how they can help us bring Montessori into our daily lives.

1. Follow the child

> "It is the child's way of learning. This is the path he follows. He learns everything without knowing he is learning it . . . treading always in the paths of joy and love."
>
> —Dr. Maria Montessori, *The Absorbent Mind*

We have already talked about how important it is to let the child lead, to not interrupt when the child is focusing deeply on something (as much as possible, at least), and to follow their interests. But I don't think it can be repeated too many times. This is the root of the Montessori approach.

This may mean that we choose to go for a walk and let the child lead. We stop and go at their pace.

It may mean that we talk about lighthouses a lot, go and visit lighthouses, read books about lighthouses, and make a model lighthouse with our child if that is their current area of interest.

It may mean getting things ready in the evening if our child is not a morning person.

Following the child means following their unique timeline, seeing where they are today, and not imposing our idea of what they should be learning when.

Let me be clear. **Following the child is not permissiveness, allowing them to do whatever they like.** We will set limits when needed, ensuring the safety and care of themselves, their environment, and others.

But it is not being directive either. When we hear ourselves giving commands, giving lessons, or giving too much information, may we remember, *Ah, yes. How can I find a way to step back and let them lead?*

We do have to do things, though, we often think. *We have to get dressed; we have to get to day care; we have to have dinner; we have to have a bath.* We will still make these things happen, but in a way that allows us to "follow the child." We can learn to work with our child rather than doing something to them like bribing, threatening, or punishing them. We will look into ways we can set limits and cultivate cooperation with our toddler in chapter 6.

2. Encourage hands-on learning

Toddlers learn best when they touch things, smell things, hear things, taste things, and see things. To raise curious learners, look for ways to provide hands-on, firsthand experiences for them.

When they start to ask questions, instead of simply giving them the answer, we can say, "I don't know. Let's find out together." Then we might be able to do a small experiment or explore together, like getting out a magnifying glass to let them take a closer look. Or, we may visit the zoo, go to the library to find some books, or ask a neighbor who knows more about the topic.

Our toddlers are learning that if they don't know something, they can be resourceful and find it out, often in a hands-on, concrete way.

At home, they will explore their environment by touching and feeling things. Instead of saying, "No, don't touch," we can observe the skill they are practicing and look for a way to redirect it toward an activity that is more appropriate. If they are taking the books off the bookshelf, we can put them back so they can practice it again and again. Or, if we don't feel like playing that game, we can think of other things they can empty, like a collection of scarves in a basket. When we find them exploring our wallet and taking out all our cards and cash, we can prepare some other containers in a basket for them to open and close and find things inside. In our classroom we even have an old wallet with some of my old loyalty cards and library cards.

Again, nature is a great place for hands-on and sensorial learning, from the wind or sun on their face, to the sand or soil in their fingers, to the sound of the waves or the crunch of the leaves, to the smell of the sea or the leaves in the woods.

3. Include the child in daily life

Toddlers are curious about what we are up to. They want to be a significant member of the family. They are not just trying to drive us crazy by clinging to our leg.

In chapter 3, we looked at many practical day-to-day activities in which we can include our toddlers.

Maybe we get them to help with food preparation. We can invite them by saying, "We are getting dinner ready. Which part would you like to do?" They can hand us things, or we can get a stepladder for them to join us in the kitchen, have an apron on a hook that they can wear, get them to wash their hands, have them tear some lettuce for the salad, have them rinse the leaves. Let them wander off if they lose interest.

Rather than thinking, *I have to do the laundry*, we can think of it as an activity to do together. I remember when my son was a toddler, I would hold him up so he could reach the buttons for the washing machine. He would often help me unload the items and then play around with the clothespins as I hung up the clothes. (There could be a low clothesline where children can hang clothes, too). We were lucky to be living in Australia at the time, where we had space for an outdoor clothesline. My daughter would lie on a little mat and kick around and watch us as we all chatted. Some days it nearly looked like domestic bliss. Most days it looked a bit more like organized chaos, but it was a lot of fun.

Having young children involved does mean that it's messier and slower. But we are making connections and memories that will last a lifetime. Those of us struggling with fitting this into our days and weeks with work and life commitments can start with moments when we do have time. This might mean setting aside an hour or two each weekend when you stay home and do laundry together, or a baking project, or care for the plants and garden. Recognize that on weekdays, we may not have the time or patience to let our children help cook, but they can be involved in setting the table, pouring their own drink at dinner, and taking their plate to the counter after the meal. We can start with the things we enjoy the most and would love to do with our children.

For more ideas, revisit the list of "practical life activities" in chapter 3 or the activities list in the appendix.

4. Go slow

> "Be fast when it makes sense to be fast, and be slow when slowness is called for. Seek to live at what musicians call the tempo giusto—the right speed."
>
> —Carl Honoré, *In Praise of Slow*

With toddlers, the "tempo giusto" will often be a lot slower than we are used to. Toddlers do not like to rush (except if they see a large open space, and then they will need to run).

Stop and look at the cracks on the pavement together, and enjoy the process rather than the product. Going slowly gives our child time to explore and be curious. And we would do well to learn from them. They remind us to slow down and be present. We can let go of making mental checklists and worrying about the past or future, too.

If we want their cooperation, we are well advised to go slowly. This means practicing not saying, "We're late again!" every morning. We will stress them out. They will resist. We will be even later. (Some ideas on how not to be late are on page 142.)

If we live more slowly, then in those occasional times when we need to rush—for example, to catch a bus or because we missed our morning alarm—our child will be a lot more accommodating. When rushed every day, our child may tune out our requests when we really need their help.

5. Help me to help myself

"Help me to help myself" is an expression often used in Montessori. It means:

- setting up things for our child to be successful by themselves
- **stepping in as little as possible and as much as is necessary**, then stepping back for our child to continue to try
- allowing time to practice
- showing our acceptance and support

How to teach our child skills

Break the task into **small steps** and show them **very slowly**. Toddlers will pick it up faster if we **don't talk** at the same time we're showing them. Simply say, "Look!" and demonstrate with slow, clear movements.

Scaffold skills

I love how Montessori materials in a classroom build on each other as the child works through them from simple to more complex, each skill building on the next.

We can apply the same principle to teaching our child to do things themselves at home. We scaffold skills as the child gains competence and maturity. The skills will become more difficult or have more steps or require them to follow multistep instructions.

For example, first we can show them how to put their foot in their shoe. Next we can show them how to pull the Velcro to tighten the shoes. Once they master that, they can learn to push down on the Velcro to fasten them. Then we invite them to put on their shoes all by themselves.

Allow time

When we allow enough time in our daily routine, we can help children help themselves. For example, we can let them get dressed at their own pace. That doesn't mean allowing unlimited time, but it might mean allowing ten to fifteen minutes while we sit on the floor with a cup of tea nearby, so we can relax and enjoy the process of helping our child learn to get dressed.

We can also practice on a rainy day, for example, letting our toddler take off their socks and put them back on, and take them off and put them back on.

These daily activities can provide moments of connection and opportunities for learning, when our child learns to do things for themselves and becomes confident in their own abilities.

If we start to feel frustrated when it is taking too long, rather than getting irritated, we can acknowledge that this time we are going to help them, and try again tomorrow.

Be friendly about mistakes

> "Nothing can take away initiative as fast as when we redo something that they did."
>
> —Jean K. Miller/Marianne White Dunlap, *The Power of Conscious Parenting*

Mistakes are simply opportunities to learn. Our children will make mistakes, break and spill things, and even hurt someone sometimes. Or when they offer to help, they may not do the task as well as we would have done it ourselves.

Instead of punishing, lecturing, or correcting them, try this:

1. If they get the name of something wrong, we can make a mental note that they don't know it yet. We can teach it again at another (neutral) time. They will be more open to learning it later than they will if we correct them. In Montessori we have a phrase for this: **"Teach by teaching, not by correcting."**
2. If they break or spill things, we can have supplies at the ready for them to help clean it up.
3. We can support them while they make it up to someone they have hurt.
4. We can model not taking ourselves too seriously when we make mistakes and show them that we apologize. "I'm sorry. What I should have said is . . ." or "What I should have done is . . ."

Offering help

Rather than rushing in to help our toddler, we wait to see how much they can manage themselves. If they are stuck or the task is difficult or new, we can offer help.

"Would you like me or someone else to help you do that?"
"Would you like to see how I do it?"
"Have you tried . . . ?"

Then we help only if they want it.

6. Encourage creativity

> "The more experience a child has with real purposeful activity and solving problems, the more useful, creative, and effective her imagination will become."
>
> —Susan Stephenson, *The Joyful Child*

There is a common misconception that the Montessori approach does not support and encourage children's creativity and imagination. Reasons cited include the fact that Montessori materials are for a specific purpose rather than being more open-ended, that we do not have a pretend-play corner in our classrooms, and that we do not encourage fantasy in children under 6 years old (rather, we focus on the concrete world around them).

Imagination is different from fantasy

Fantasy means making up something that does not exist in reality. Children under 6 don't easily perceive the difference between something that is made up and something that is real. In a research study, "Do Monsters Dream? Young Children's Understanding of the Fantasy/Reality Distinction" by Tanya Sharon and Jacqueline D. Woolley, young children were shown fantastical and natural pictures of animals. The 3-year-olds had difficulty distinguishing real from fantastical scenes.

We may witness this when a child is scared by something in books or other media, from dragons and monsters to images they see on the news. It can feel very real to them.

Imagination, on the other hand, is used when our mind takes the information we have collected and comes up with creative possibilities. In Montessori, we lay the foundation for our child in the first years in reality, planting the seeds for their life as creative and imaginative citizens of the world. To establish a strong foundation, we can provide our children with hands-on experiences in the real world in the early years. Around 2.5+ years, we will see our child begin with pretend play. This is a sign that they are processing what they see around them (imagination). They play families, bake us cookies, and pretend to be the schoolteacher. They are being creative without becoming overwhelmed by the idea of dragons, monsters, or other things they can't see or experience directly (fantasy).

When providing materials for such play, we can keep the items less prescriptive—scarves and other objects can be used in many ways, whereas a firefighter's suit can be used in only one way.

The focus on reality won't limit their creativity; it will enhance it. We can see the groundwork flourish in adolescence when the imagination becomes particularly strong and they start to come up with creative solutions to our world problems and for social change.

What about artistic creativity?

As we discussed in chapter 4, we can provide a rich and inviting area for artistic creativity. We can:

- Set up beautiful materials at our child's height.
- Create invitations for creativity—beautiful trays with age-appropriate materials to explore.
- Make beauty part of our home, including art and plants, which they will absorb and be inspired by.
- Choose quality over quantity when it comes to the materials.

In addition, there are key principles that we can practice to support our child's development of their artistic creativity. We can:

- Invite open-ended use of materials (use fewer art kits and coloring books, which are more prescriptive).
- Prepare ourselves to encourage creativity—allow time and be open to allowing mess and exploration; prepare a space that is okay to get dirty; relax, join in, and create together.
- Ask, not tell. Rather than instructing our child, we can encourage exploration.
- Allow boredom. When we have unscheduled time in our day to sit without anything planned (and without technology to entertain us), our child has a chance to be bored. Their mind can wander and daydream, they can come up with new ideas, and they can make new connections. When the mind is bored, it seeks stimulation and becomes increasingly creative.
- Look at the process, not the result. Focus on our child's effort by describing their effort. "You made big circles." "I see you mixed these two colors."
- Show our child that there are no mistakes in this work. We can experiment and learn when things don't turn out the way we expected.

Most of all we can have fun inspiring, exploring, and creating with our child.

7. Observation

Often Montessori teachers will tell parents, "Just observe your child." *Observe what about my child? Why? And how?*

Observing is seeing or perceiving without any judgment or analysis. It means being just like a video camera, which objectively records the situation and doesn't analyze what is being seen.

For example, a Montessori teacher might make the following observation about a student: "John releases the pencil from his right hand. It falls to the ground. He looks out the window. He transfers his weight from the left foot to the right foot. He bends his knees. He picks up the pencil using his thumb and index finger of the right hand."

By observing, we are scientifically recording what we see rather than rushing to react or making any assumptions. **With the information, we can respond rather than react.**

We see more details, we notice when something changes, and we practice taking the judgment away from what we see. It allows us to see the child with fresh eyes every day.

What to do with these observations?

These observations will help in many ways.

We learn to see that our child is developing in their own unique way. We are able to follow their interests and keep them curious about the world around them.

We may hold back before stepping in, seeing opportunities instead of limiting their curiosity and creativity. And we also see those occasions when we need to step in calmly to keep them safe.

When we observe over a period of time, we will begin to observe subtle differences about our child that we might otherwise miss.

We can also identify factors in the environment or with the adults that help or hinder independence, movement, communication, or other areas of development.

Observing helps us support our children to be the curious learners they are. Observing enables us to look at our child clearly and without judgment or a preconceived idea of what they are capable of.

SOME THINGS WE CAN OBSERVE

FINE-MOTOR SKILLS

- How they grasp and hold objects
- Which fingers and which hand they use
- The grip they use on a paintbrush or pencil
- Which fine-motor skill activities and skills they are practicing, such as using their pincer grip, threading, and so on

GROSS-MOTOR SKILLS

- How they come to stand or sit
- How they walk—distance of legs or arm movements
- Balance
- The gross-motor skills they are practicing
- Whether they choose activities that use gross-motor skills
- Whether the environment helps or hinders their movement

COMMUNICATION

- Sounds/words they make to communicate
- Smiling
- Crying—intensity, duration
- Other body language
- How they express themselves
- Eye contact during conversations
- Language used
- How they are responded to when they communicate

COGNITIVE DEVELOPMENT

- What they are interested in
- What they are practicing and learning to master, and the activities they can complete
- How long they play with an activity

SOCIAL DEVELOPMENT

- Interactions with others—peers and adults
- Whether they observe others
- How they ask for help
- How they provide assistance to others

EMOTIONAL DEVELOPMENT

- When the child cries, smiles, and laughs
- How they get comforted or comfort themselves
- How they respond to strangers
- How they deal with moments of separation
- How they manage when things do not go their way

EATING

- What they eat and how much
- Whether they are passive or active eaters—being fed or feeding themselves

SLEEPING

- Any sleep patterns
- How they fall asleep
- Quality of sleep
- Position during sleep
- How they transition to waking

INDEPENDENCE

- Signs of independence
- Relationship to adults

CLOTHING

- Whether the clothing helps or hinders movement and independence
- Whether they try to put on and take off their own clothing
- Whether they express preferences for their clothing

SELF-OBSERVATION

- Record our communication—what we say and how we interact with our child
- If anything comes up for us as we observe our child
- How we respond if our child does not eat or sleep
- What we say when our child does something we like or don't like

INGREDIENTS AND PRINCIPLES FOR ENCOURAGING CURIOSITY

FIVE INGREDIENTS

1. Trust in the child
2. A rich learning environment
3. Time
4. A safe and secure base
5. Fostering a sense of wonder

SEVEN PRINCIPLES

1. Follow the child
2. Encourage hands-on learning
3. Include the child in daily life
4. Go slow
5. Help me to help myself
6. Encourage creativity
7. Observation

PART TWO

ACCEPTING OUR CHILD FOR WHO THEY ARE

Toddlers want to feel significant, they want to feel like they belong, and they want to be accepted for who they are. If we understand this, we can move away from doing battle with them or being triggered by them, and move toward being able to guide, support, and lead them.

GIVE TODDLERS SIGNIFICANCE, BELONGING, AND ACCEPTANCE FOR WHO THEY ARE

Seeing the world through our toddler's eyes helps us **see their perspective**. This is similar to empathizing with, or having compassion for, our child. Whichever we choose, we recognize that everyone is right in their own eyes.

If our child grabs a toy out of another child's hands, they are not trying to be naughty. If we look at it from their perspective, we can see they simply want to play with that toy *right now*. Then we can observe them, see if they need any help, or be ready to step in if needed.

We may think our child is being destructive because they are pulling the soil from the potted plants, but when we look from their perspective, we can understand that they are seeing something in their environment at their height that needs to be explored *right now*. We can observe them and decide if we need to step in to remove the plant or perhaps cover the soil.

Instead of thinking that our child is trying to wind us up by poking out their tongue at us and then laughing, we can look from their perspective. They are testing out a new sound, seeing our reaction, and figuring out cause and effect. Again, let's observe and see if they stop all by themselves. Or we may come up with something else that is okay and say something like "I don't like it when you poke your tongue out at me, but we can go and tumble on the carpet over here."

When we stop to observe and remove the judgment, it opens us up to be able to see our child and accept them for who they are.

When we ask, "How can I get my child to be less shy/concentrate more/be more interested in art/be more active?" and so on, we are not accepting them for who they are. Instead, we can work to show our child we love them just as they are, where they are right now. Really, that is what anyone wants.

Significance. Belonging. Acceptance for who we are.

BE THEIR TRANSLATOR

When we can see things from our child's perspective, we can also be their translator when needed, as though we're looking up what they are trying to say in a dictionary.

"Are you trying to tell me . . . ?" is a useful phrase for translating the toddler's needs into words.

When they throw their food on the floor, we can say, "Are you trying to tell me you're all finished?"

We can also use this for an older child who is calling people names or acting inappropriately. "It sounds like you are pretty angry right now. Are you trying to say you don't like it when they touch your things?"

And we could translate for our partner or the child's grandparent if we notice they are getting upset. "It sounds like it is important to your mother/grandfather to sit at the table to eat, and you really want to walk around with your food."

SOMETIMES OUR JOB IS TO BE OUR CHILD'S **TRANSLATOR**

ALLOW ALL FEELINGS, BUT NOT ALL BEHAVIOR

We might think, *If I accept them for who they are, see things from their perspective, and allow all their feelings, do I have to accept all their behavior?*

This is absolutely not the case. We step in if necessary to stop any inappropriate behavior. As the adult, we often need to act as our toddler's prefrontal cortex (the rational part of their brain), which is still developing. We can step in to keep them safe. To keep others safe. To keep ourselves safe. To show them they can disagree with others in a respectful way. To show them how to show up and be responsible human beings.

Examples:

"It's okay to disagree, but I can't let you hurt your brother/sister. You sit on this side of me, and you sit on the other."

"I can't let you hurt me/I can't let you speak to me that way/I cannot let you hurt yourself. But I see something important is going on, and I am trying to understand."

GIVE OUR CHILD FEEDBACK

—INSTEAD OF PRAISE

Montessori teachers like to help children build their own sense of self, learn how to accept themselves for who they are, and learn what feels good in the way they treat others.

Since the 1970s and '80s, there has been a big push for parents to praise their child to build the child's self-esteem. So we hear parents saying, "good job," "good boy," "good girl." In Dutch, they even have a phrase: "*goed zo.*" We say it in response to everything. We praise children for their paintings, for flushing the toilet, we applaud them, and we declare every physical feat a triumph.

These types of praise are extrinsic motivators that do not come from within the child themselves.

Alfie Kohn wrote a useful article, "Five Reasons to Stop Saying 'Good Job!'" in which he points out that:

- Praise can actually be used to manipulate children when we use it as a bargaining tool to motivate them.
- It can create praise junkies.
- Praise can actually take the joy away, with children looking to us for reassurance rather than experiencing delight at what they have achieved.
- Children can become less motivated when they do something for praise, because it removes the meaning for themselves.
- Praise can lower achievement—when an activity is tied to the pressure to perform, the child's interest or pleasure in the activity goes down, or they take fewer risks.

Montessori teachers believe instead that a child will learn to behave if we help to develop their intrinsic motivation—their internal radar that tells them that something is right (or wrong) and recognizes what helps (or hurts) themselves or someone else.

What we can say instead . . .

It can be surprising at first how often we find ourselves saying "good job." When we start to be conscious of it, we can choose to change it. When looking for alternatives, the best guide is to think about what we would say to another adult when **giving them feedback**.

Here are some ideas that I first learned from the book *How to Talk So Kids Will Listen and Listen So Kids Will Talk* by Adele Faber and Elaine Mazlish. What I love about these suggestions is that they let the child know more specifically what we appreciate and give the child vocabulary that is so much richer than simply "good job."

1. Describe what we see

Focus on the process rather than the product and describe what our child has done. Give feedback by using positive and factual descriptions of the child's actions and accomplishments.

"You took your plate to the kitchen."
"You look really pleased with yourself."
"You got dressed all by yourself."
"You put the blocks in the basket and put them back on the shelf."
"You used blue and red paint. I see a swirl over here."

2. Sum it up with a word

"You packed your bag and are ready to go to the beach. Now, that's what I call *independence*!"
"You helped your grandma with her bag. Now, that's what I call being *thoughtful*."
"You wiped up the water on the floor with the mop without me asking. That's what I call being *resourceful*."

3. Describe how we feel

"I am so excited for you."
"It's a pleasure to walk into the living room when everything has been put away."

ROLES AND LABELS

Another part of accepting a child for who they are means seeing them without any preconceived judgments or ideas about them.

As the adults in their lives, we need to be careful about labeling our children.

We likely have someone in our life who has been labeled "the clown," "the shy one," "the naughty one." Even positive labels can be difficult to always live up to (e.g., "the clever one," "the athletic one").

These labels can last a lifetime—something the child never grows out of.

Instead, we can give them **another view of themselves**. Recall stories with them of times when they have been successful in difficult areas. Let them overhear us tell someone how they worked hard to overcome an obstacle. For example, we can say, "I liked watching you carry that glass so carefully to the table with two hands," to a child who might otherwise be labeled clumsy.

Labels are commonly used with siblings, too. Once a new baby is born into the family, a young child suddenly becomes the "big brother/sister." It is a huge responsibility to have to behave all the time and show their sibling how to be a "big kid." Instead of always leaving the eldest in charge, for example, while we are in the bathroom, we can **get children to look after each other**, regardless of their age. We can make sure that younger children also take on age-appropriate responsibilities rather than leaving everything to the eldest.

Let's see our toddler and accept them for who they are. In moments of celebration. And when they are having a hard time. Every day.

Allowing our child to be curious and giving them a sense of significance, belonging, and acceptance provides a **solid foundation of connection and trust** with our child—something we will need to cultivate cooperation and when we have to set limits with them.

Without connection, we get very little cooperation; without trust, setting limits becomes difficult.

TO PRACTICE

1. How can we allow our child to be more curious?
   - Does our child feel we trust them?
   - Is there a rich learning environment?
   - Do we allow time to let them explore and to go at their own pace?
   - Is it physically and psychologically safe for them?
   - How can we foster a sense of wonder?
2. Practice observing our child for ten to fifteen minutes a day.
   - Be curious
   - Be objective
   - Avoid analysis
3. How can we give our child a sense of significance and belonging, and let them know we accept them for who they are?
   - See from their perspective
   - Translate for them
   - Give them feedback rather than praise
   - Avoid roles and labels

NURTURING COOPERATION AND RESPONSIBILITY IN OUR CHILD

6

PART ONE

CULTIVATING COOPERATION

PART TWO

SETTING LIMITS

PART ONE

CULTIVATING COOPERATION

WHEN YOUR CHILD WON'T LISTEN TO YOU

Cultivating cooperation in a toddler is a tricky thing. Toddlers are naturally curious, they are impulsive, and they are servants to their will. Common ways of trying to get cooperation from toddlers include threats, bribes, punishment, and constant repetition.

We find ourselves thinking, *Why won't they listen to me?*

> "If you've told a child a thousand times, and the child still has not learned, then it is not the child who is the slow learner."
>
> —Walter B. Barbe

WHY THE MONTESSORI APPROACH DOES NOT USE THREATS, BRIBES, OR PUNISHMENTS

The word *discipline* comes from the Latin word *disciplina*, meaning "teaching; learning." So we should consider **what we are teaching our children and what our children are learning** from the way we discipline them.

Threats, bribes, and punishments are extrinsic motivations. The child may cooperate to avoid a punishment or to get a sticker or some ice cream. But that kind of discipline rarely has a long-term effect. It is a quick fix, if it works at all. It can also be a distraction from the issue at hand.

I once got a detention at school for writing a mean note about the teacher (in my defense she was scary, but I should never have called her a dragon). Of course, the teacher found the note. I was so upset about getting a detention that I told everyone in the class that the teacher was mean. Did the punishment work? Not at all. Instead of being sorry that I had wronged the teacher, I felt that the teacher was the one who had done something wrong.

When we threaten a child with punishment like a time-out, we begin to erode the trust between parent and child. Two things can happen. They can become scared of the adult and cooperate out of fear, or they find a way to do what they want sneakily, without their parent finding out.

Similarly, threats and bribes may get the child to cooperate, but not because the child wants to help us. They simply want to avoid the negative consequences (punishment) or take advantage of the positive ones (rewards). Threats and bribes may need to get bigger and more elaborate as the child grows. If they have learned to do something only so they'll get a sticker, the "price" of their cooperation will rise.

These methods of getting our toddler to cooperate are exhausting. They place all the responsibility on us, the adult. We are thinking, *How am I going to get my child to get dressed/eat/wash their hands?* We end up nagging, and the child stops listening to us altogether.

There is an another approach.

Each time we are challenged by our child, we can see it as a teaching opportunity for us and a learning opportunity for them.

Let's add to our toolbox for cultivating cooperation and look for ways to work with our child to get them to cooperate (without losing our cool).

And let's ask ourselves, *How can I support my child right now?*

Cultivating cooperation involves:

- problem solving with our toddler
- involving the child
- talking in a way that helps them listen
- managing our expectations
- a little bonus

Note: We'll need a foundation of connection and trust with our toddler to get their cooperation. So when everything seems like a battle, it's good to go back and review the ideas from the last chapter.

PROBLEM SOLVING WITH OUR TODDLERS

I like to start by finding a way to work with the child so they feel like they have some control over the situation. Even though they are small, toddlers want to be involved in how things happen.

The child is not in charge, but they can have input into how to solve problems. We can ask, **"How can we solve the problem?"** and then come up with solutions together.

We might be coming up with most of the ideas, but the toddler is learning the process. Don't underestimate them. Sometimes they will come up with great ideas (often much more creative than ours).

- "You want to stay at the park and I'm ready to leave. I wonder how we can solve the problem."
- "You'd like to finish that puzzle and then you'll put on your shirt? Okay, I'll go and get dressed and come back to see if you'd like some help."
- "Two kids and one toy. I wonder how you'll work that out."

Even a preverbal child can help. For example, if a crawling sibling has taken one of their toys, they might come up with the idea to bring their sibling another toy to play with.

If it's a bigger problem, we can write a list of solutions. Include even silly ideas if they come up. Then we can review the list together and find solutions that everyone can live with. We can select one to try and set a time to come back to see if it is working or needs to be adjusted a little. This process may not be quite so formal with a toddler, but they are learning a practice that we can build on as they get older.

In addition, the toddler is more likely to take ownership of the planned solution and follow through. It's also a great skill for solving problems with others. (This is an idea to come back to when we talk about siblings in chapter 7.)

When we get our toddlers involved in solving problems, we may even find we are more relaxed. We get to share a little of the responsibility. We remain open and curious about how it might happen in a way we may not expect, without forcing it.

Making a checklist with our child

One way to solve problems with toddlers is to make a simple checklist with them (especially one with pictures).

If they resist getting dressed in the morning, we can make a morning routine chart of all the steps they need to do to get ready. If bedtime is difficult, the list will include all the things they need to do before bed, including drinking some water and using the toilet.

We can draw pictures of each step or take photos of them and print them out. If they want to change the order each day, we can make sticky notes for each step or laminate some pictures with Velcro on the back.

Then we can check the chart to see what we need to do next. That way it's the chart doing the work, not us. "Can you see what is next on the list?" or "The checklist says we brush our teeth next."

When they are involved in making and using the checklist, they take ownership of the solution.

GOOD MORNING CHECKLIST

MAKE BED

EAT BREAKFAST

GET DRESSED

BRUSH HAIR

BRUSH TEETH

SHOES/COAT ON

GOOD NIGHT CHECKLIST

EAT DINNER

BATH

PAJAMAS ON

BRUSH TEETH

DRINK WATER

USE TOILET/CHANGE DIAPER

STORY TIME

CUDDLES

SLEEP TIME

WAYS TO INVOLVE OUR CHILD

Give age-appropriate choices

We can offer our toddler choices to encourage cooperation. Not big decisions like where they will go to school, but age-appropriate choices, like which color T-shirt they would like to wear (out of two seasonally appropriate options); or when they are heading to the bath, we can offer them the option of jumping like a kangaroo or walking on all fours sideways like a crab.

This gives the toddler a sense of control over the situation and involves them in the process.

Note: Some toddlers do not like choices. Just as with any of these suggestions, use the ones that work for the child and leave the rest.

Give them information

Rather than issuing commands—"Put the orange peel in the bin, please"—we can give information instead: "The orange peel goes in the bin." Then they can figure out for themselves that they need to take it to the bin. It becomes something they choose to do rather than another order from the adult.

Use one word

Sometimes we use too many words to give instructions to our children. "We are going to the park. We'll need to get our shoes. Our shoes protect our feet. It's good to put them on. Where are your shoes? Did you put them on yet?" And on and on it goes.

Try using just one word. "Shoes." Again the child needs to figure out what they need to do on their own, giving them some control in the situation.

We are also modeling respectful communication to our children. And they will pick this up. One day my family was leaving the house, and we were all putting on our coats and shoes by the front door—a pretty tight spot. My son (around 7 at the time) said to me, "Mum. Laces." I looked down, and indeed I was standing on his shoelace. He could have rolled his eyes at me and said, "Mummmm, do you have to stand on my laces?" or worse.

It's another reminder that what we *do* speaks louder than what we *tell* them.

Get their agreement

Getting our child on board and letting them feel like they're part of the process will help with gaining their cooperation. If we know that our child has trouble leaving the house or the playground, we can let them know we'll be leaving in five minutes. We can then **check to make sure they heard and make a plan with them**. They may not understand exactly how long five minutes is, but they learn the concept over time.

We could say, "I see you are working on this puzzle, and we are leaving in five minutes. I'm worried you might not have time to finish it before we leave. Do you want to put it somewhere safe to keep working on it when we get back, or do you want to put it away and do it later?"

At the playground, we could say, "We have five minutes before we leave the playground. What would you like to have one last turn on?"

I don't love using an alarm to remind a child (used a lot, this could become an extrinsic motivator). However, used from time to time it can be an effective way to get their agreement, especially if they are involved in helping to set the timer. And, just like a checklist, it's the timer that tells them the time is up, not us.

HOW WE CAN TALK TO HELP THEM LISTEN

Use positive language

Instead of telling a child *what not to do*, we can tell them with positive language *what they can do* instead. Rather than, "No running" (what they should not do), we can say, "We walk inside" (what we would like them to do).

Instead of, "No, don't climb," we can say, "You can keep your feet on the floor or you can go outside to climb."

If we tell our toddler, "Stop yelling!" we may also be raising our voice. First, they will mirror us and shout back; second, they will hear precisely what we don't want them to do. Instead we could say (perhaps in a whisper), "Let's use our quiet voices."

Speak with a respectful tone and attitude

Our tone of voice is a way to show our toddlers that we respect them. A whiny tone, an insecure voice, a strict voice, or a threatening tone can distort the best of intentions and does not show our child we value them and want to work with them.

If we can remember, it is helpful to check in with our voice and whether we are coming from a calm place in our heart. (See chapter 8 for ways to calm ourselves down.) We can even use a whisper now and then. Our toddler's ears are sure to prick up.

Ask them for help

Toddlers want to be involved, so if we would like our child to come inside, we might be able to ask for their help in carrying the keys or a heavy bag. At the supermarket, we can get them to help by making a visual shopping list, which they can be in charge of (we can cut out pictures from a food magazine together or draw simple pictures); let them take the items off the shelf; or put them on the conveyer belt at the register.

Say "yes"

If we are saying "no" a hundred times a day, our child will gradually begin to ignore it altogether. It is best to reserve "no" for times when their safety is a concern.

Instead of saying "no" to set a limit, we can generally find an alternative way to express what we want to say by actually agreeing with them and saying "yes."

Say a toddler wants another cracker but they haven't finished their first one. We could say in a gentle tone, "Yes, you can have another cracker . . . when you have finished this one." Or maybe if there are none left, "Yes, you can have more . . . when we go to the store. Let's write it on our shopping list."

It takes some time to break this habit. It can be useful to note down all the times we say "no" and then brainstorm (perhaps with a friend) some more positive ways to respond next time.

Use humor

Children respond well to humor, and it is a lighthearted way to encourage cooperation.

Sometimes when I've been helping a child get dressed and they are resisting, I pretend to put their shoe on my foot. The child laughs and tells me, "No, Simone, it goes on my foot." And they put it on.

Humor is particularly useful when we are on the verge of losing our temper. Something as simple as singing a silly song can relieve some tension for us and coax a smile from them. It's a simple way to start fresh.

If our child is going through a "no" phase, adjust our language

It is easy to know when a toddler is in this phase. Ask them if they need to use the toilet, if they will get dressed, if they want chocolate, and they'll just say "no."

During the "no" phase, we may want to adjust our language to tell them what is happening, rather than asking them. We might say, "It's time to eat/have a bath/leave the park." This can still be done with respect, using a gentle voice and kind words, but as their leader.

Show them

Sometimes we might need to actually get up to show them what they need to do rather than repeating ourselves from the other side of the room. If they are still not sure what to do with the orange peel, we could go over to the bin and physically touch or point to it, saying, "It goes in here." Show them.

Actions speak louder than words.

MANAGING EXPECTATIONS

Have age-appropriate expectations and be prepared

We cannot expect our toddler to behave in the way we like all of the time. Sitting quietly in a doctor's waiting room or in a cafe or on a train can be very difficult. Remember that they have a strong will to explore, move, and communicate, and are very impulsive. This is not meant to excuse their behavior. However, it does mean we can prepare ourselves.

First, we may need to adjust our expectations—we may not get to read a magazine, check our phone, or make a phone call. In a cafe or restaurant, be prepared to take them for a little walk when they start to get agitated or loud, perhaps to see the chef at work or look at the fish tank together. Waiting for a plane, we can stand at the window of the airport and watch all the action happening outside to prepare the plane for departure.

Second, be prepared. Don't forget to pack plenty of water, food, a few favorite books, and a little zippered pouch with a few favorite toys—a couple of small vehicles, a bottle with a coin to drop in, some shells, and so on. If there are any delays wherever we may be, we will be prepared to support our child and help them cooperate.

Try to wait until they have finished their task before making a request

If a toddler is busy working on a puzzle and we ask them to get ready to leave, they often won't respond. We may think, *They never listen to me!*

When I put myself in a similar situation—perhaps someone interrupts me while I am right in the middle of answering an email—it can be irritating. I just want to finish what I am doing, and then I can give 100 percent of my attention.

So if we want our child to come eat their lunch or to remind them to use the toilet, whenever possible, we can try to wait until they have finished what they are working on and then ask them before they start the next thing.

Allow time for processing

It can take a toddler (and older children, too) a while to process what we say.

Maybe we ask them to put on their pajamas and get no response. We can try counting slowly to ten in our head. Not aloud. This is for our benefit, to help us wait for them to process what we have said.

By the time I get up to three or four, I would definitely have repeated myself already, and by seven, I would have asked another time. By the time I get to eight or nine, often I find that the child is starting to respond.

It's not that they aren't listening; they are just processing what we said.

Keep a daily rhythm

Do not underestimate how much a toddler likes having the same rhythm every day. We can use that to manage expectations: wake up, get dressed, eat breakfast, leave the house, lunchtime, nap time, dinnertime, bath time, get ready for bed. It does not have to be on a fixed schedule, but the more regular the routine, the less resistance we will get. (See chapter 7 for more on daily rhythm.)

BONUS

Write a note

Most toddlers can't read yet, but notes can still be very powerful. We can write a note that says "No climbing" and place it on the table. Then we can point to the note and say, "It says, 'No climbing.'" If it is written down, it gives a certain weight and authority to the message. It is the sign setting the rule rather than the adult having to repeat the rule. And it is always consistent.

We can use a note in the kitchen if the oven is at the toddler's height. When we turn on the oven, we can show our child that we are putting up a note saying "HOT" to remind them the oven is on and dangerous to touch.

Notes are very effective, even with prereaders. But use them in moderation. If notes are stuck everywhere, they will definitely lose their effectiveness.

Another way to use notes is to keep a notebook. If our child is upset about leaving or something is not going their way, we can write it down in a notebook and perhaps draw a picture. This acknowledges to the child that we have heard them. Sometimes that is all they need.

IDEAS FOR CULTIVATING COOPERATION

PROBLEM SOLVING WITH OUR TODDLER

- Ask, "How can we solve the problem?"
- Make a checklist.

INVOLVE THE CHILD

- Give age-appropriate choices.
- Give them information.
- Use one word.
- Get their agreement.

TALK IN A WAY THAT HELPS THEM LISTEN

- Use positive language.
- Speak with a respectful tone and attitude.
- Ask them for help.
- Say "yes."
- Use humor.
- If our child is going through a "no" phase, adjust our language.
- Show them.

MANAGE EXPECTATIONS

- Have age-appropriate expectations and be prepared.
- Try to wait until they have finished before making a request.
- Allow time for processing.
- Keep a daily rhythm.

BONUS

- Write a note.

PART TWO

SETTING LIMITS

HELPING OUR CHILD TAKE RESPONSIBILITY

Cooperation can be cultivated without resorting to threats, bribes, and punishments. But if our child is still not cooperating, then it's time to learn about setting limits.

This is the most difficult part of caring for a toddler in a Montessori way. We want to give them as much freedom as possible to explore so they remain curious, but within limits to keep them safe, to teach them to respect others, and to establish our own boundaries.

In the Netherlands, I notice that the Dutch people (generally speaking, of course) seem to do this very naturally. I don't see many Dutch parents or caregivers getting into a battle with their toddler or having exchanges that end up with the adult shouting at them. From time to time, I see a young child crying on the back of their parent's bike, yet the parent remains calm, continuing where they need to go, and offering some comforting words to the child.

I'm going to show how to do the same, to set limits in a respectful way for both the child and the rest of the family.

It will take some practice. We are basically learning a new language. It can be easier to learn if we are able to get support from other people raising their children in a similar way so we can learn from one another and discuss tricky moments. And when we get it wrong, we can remind one another that we are doing our best and use it as an opportunity to apologize to our child.

IT'S OKAY TO SET LIMITS

When my children were small, I thought my job was simply to make them happy. To be honest, that's the easy part. As parents we are here to help them deal with *all* life will throw at them: to be there to celebrate with them, to help them deal with moments of disappointment and grief—the good and the bad.

Sometimes we need to set limits. To keep them safe. To show them how to be respectful. To step in when they are not making a positive choice. To help them grow into responsible human beings.

Setting limits can feel difficult. Our child may not be happy with the limit being set. Yet when we set a limit in a supportive and loving way, they learn to trust that we have their best interests in mind, and the connection with our child can even grow stronger.

Difficult times make us grow. Difficult times make our children grow. And how amazing that our children know that we love them even when they are having a tantrum, pulling our hair, or refusing to get dressed.

BE CLEAR ON THE LIMITS

SET GROUND/HOUSE RULES

Children, toddlers especially, need order. They need to know what to expect. They need to know that things are consistent and predictable. That their parents will keep them safe and secure. That they will get the same answer whether their parent had a full night's sleep or the baby woke them every hour on the hour.

It's a good idea to have a few rules that are important to the family. Too many rules and it will be like a dictatorship. But it's helpful to have a few simple and clear rules aimed at keeping everyone safe and living more peacefully with others—just as we have some agreed-upon rules and laws for living together in the larger society.

How many of us already have some ground rules in our home? Maybe stuck on the fridge? Maybe a list of family values framed on the living room wall? Or maybe simply discussed between the adults of the household?

When I ask this question in my parent workshops, I find that most participants don't have any ground rules at all. That means we are mostly just winging it—making it up on the spot. This can be difficult to keep track of, for us and definitely for our toddler. Imagine if they changed the rules for traffic lights and some days the red light meant "stop" and on other days it meant "go." No wonder toddlers get mixed messages when we change our minds.

Here are some ideas for rules that we could use at home, adjusting for what works for each family:

Examples of ground/house rules

- **We are kind to each other.** This means that even if we disagree, we will not hurt each other physically or tease each other; it teaches children to respect themselves and each other.
- **We sit at the (dining) table to eat.** This is a practical rule that prevents food from going everywhere in the house. It also reminds people that eating is a social occasion and that we don't play and eat at the same time.
- **We contribute to the household.** No matter what our age, we help around the house, and our help is valued.
- **We engage in rough play by mutual consent.** This is a mouthful for young children, but they understand its meaning. If someone says "Stop," they are saying that they are not having fun anymore and the game needs to stop.

These ground/house rules provide a foundation that we can always return to. We may need to revise them as our children grow. Not in the middle of an argument, though. Do it at a neutral (ideally, planned) moment.

FOLLOW THROUGH WITH KIND AND CLEAR ACTION

> "If you say it, mean it. If you mean it, follow through with kind and firm action."
>
> —Jane Nelsen, *Positive Discipline: The First Three Years*

If, despite our best efforts to work with our child, our child refuses to cooperate, then we take **kind and clear action**.

Let's say they do not want to have their diaper changed, they are throwing their food, or they won't leave the playground. Then we **acknowledge their feelings**. But we take action. We are the leader—a respectful leader.

We touch gently if we need to handle them. We pick them up if we need to, giving a short explanation as we go. We change their diaper. We help them bring their plate to the kitchen. We leave the park. We are setting clear, loving limits for our child.

Make it logical and age appropriate

The consequence should be directly related to the behavior. Young toddlers cannot follow the logic where there is no direct relationship. It doesn't make sense to them that if they don't listen, they won't be able to go to the park or have ice cream later.

I once was on an airplane and heard a father say to his son, "If you don't behave, we will turn the plane around and go home." That's a threat that is going to be very difficult to follow through on.

Also, no stickers—seriously. That is just a bribe.

Instead, find a logical consequence. Let's say they are throwing the ball inside, and we have asked them to stop. A logical consequence would be for us to put the ball away and let our child try again later.

Let me share an example from when my children were a little older but one that gives a clear example of logical consequences and following through.

My children were around 7 and 8 years old and sitting in the *bakfiets* (a bike here in the Netherlands where there is a box in front with enough room for up to 4 children to sit). They were irritated with each other and encroaching on each other's personal space. They started stomping on each other's feet, and it was hard for me to concentrate on cycling, so I asked them to stop. When they continued, I quietly pulled my bike over to the side of the road and asked them to get out. We were going to walk until they were ready to sit in the bike calmly.

It was hard to follow through with kind and clear action. My children were pretty angry at first, but I kept an even tone. "Yes, you sound upset that we had to get out of the bike." Gradually they calmed down. After walking for a bit, I asked if they were ready to try again. I don't remember them ever stomping on each other's feet in the *bakfiets* again.

Express the limit clearly

I feel most comfortable setting limits with language like "I can't let you . . ." or "I'm going to . . ." It's clear. It takes ownership of our role as the parent. And it is respectful to both child and parent. We can also make sure they hear us by going to them and getting down to their level.

- "I can't let you take that toy out of their hands. I'm using my gentle hands to take your hands away."
- "I can't let you hit that child. I'm going to separate you."

- "I'm going to put a pillow here to protect you from hurting yourself."
- "I'm going to put you down. If you need to bite, you can bite on this apple."

No need to explain the limit every time

Once the child knows the limit, we don't need to explain it at length every time.

Let's say that our child throws food at every mealtime. We find ourselves having the same conversation over and over—how we can't let them throw food, that food is for eating, and so on. We do not need to get into a negotiation or give them lots of chances.

If the behavior continues, it's a reminder to talk less and move to kind and clear action. We can say, "It looks like you are all finished. Your plate goes in the kitchen." (See page 146 for tips on food throwing.)

Set limits for safety

If our toddler is doing something dangerous, we must step in and take them out of danger. This is the one time I say "no." This helps to get their attention when there is danger.

Some things I consider dangerous: touching something hot, going near an electrical outlet, running onto the road, getting too far ahead in the street unattended, climbing near a window.

Pick them up, say, "No, I can't let you touch that," and remove them from the area.

We may need to continue to repeat this if they keep going back. In that case I would look to see if I could change the environment to remove or hide the danger. Place a box over the power outlet, move a couch in front of wires, or move a glass cabinet to a room with a door that locks.

If they laugh

It is difficult if they laugh when we set a limit. I would still continue to follow through with kind and clear action. They may be used to getting a reaction from us. Instead, stay calm and say, for example, "You want to have fun right now, but I can't let you hurt your brother."

ACKNOWLEDGE NEGATIVE FEELINGS

They will probably be unhappy about a limit being set, so we acknowledge their feelings and see things from their perspective.

Guess their feeling

I have learned from Nonviolent Communication to guess what a child might be feeling rather than simply naming it.

- It looks like you . . .
- Are you telling me . . . ?
- Are you feeling . . . ?
- It seems like . . .
- I'm guessing you might feel . . .

Ask them if they are disappointed, make guesses about how they feel ("Are you telling me you're upset we are leaving the park?"), or describe how they look ("You look really angry right now").

You may guess the wrong feeling, but that's okay. They will just shout back something like, "I'm not!" or "I'm just disappointed." You have still helped them clarify their feelings.

Sportscasting

We can also use the sportscasting technique that I first heard about from Janet Lansbury, author of *No Bad Kids* and *Elevating Child Care*. Just as a sportscaster gives commentary about a football game, we can describe what is happening in a factual way (just as we do in observation). This can give us some emotional distance during this difficult moment, allow us to observe and name what we see, and stop us from jumping in to solve the problem.

"You are holding on to the swing. Your hands are holding tight. I'm using my gentle hands to help you let go. I'm holding you close to me as we leave the park."

Let the big feelings out

We can also acknowledge their feelings when things don't go their way, like when they want to wear something that isn't available or appropriate. Let them rage, hold them if they'll let us or keep them safe if they won't, and offer them a hug once they have calmed down.

Let them release the full range of emotions. Allow even ugly feelings. Show them we are able to love them at their worst. Once they are calm, we'll be able to help them make amends if needed.

Tip

I've noticed that once toddlers have processed their feelings and are calm, they often take a deep breath or release a big sigh. We can look for this kind of physical sign to show they are completely calm again.

DEALING WITH TANTRUMS

When a toddler has a tantrum, they are communicating that something did not go their way. They are having a hard time. They may have done something wrong, but right now, the first thing to do is **help them calm down**.

I love the analogy used in the book *The Whole-Brain Child* by Daniel Siegel and Tina Payne Bryson—when a child is upset, he "flips his lid." This means that the upstairs part of the brain—the cerebral cortex, the part of the brain that makes rational decisions and allows for self-control—is not available to the child.

Therefore, all the reasoning in the world or explanations will fall on deaf ears. We need to first help them close the lid by giving them support to calm down.

We can offer them a cuddle; we don't assume that they want one. Some children like to be cuddled to help them calm down. Some children will push us away. If they push us away, we make sure they are safe and we can offer them a cuddle when they are calm.

We are saying it's okay for them to melt down. Rather than trying to get the tantrum to stop as soon as possible, allow them to express all their feelings safely until they are calm, and show that we are there to help if they need us. And, once they are calm, we can help them make amends if needed.

That's it.

It may happen in the street, in the supermarket, in the park. That's okay. Move them out of the way (if you can). Give them the time they need to calm down. We try to stay calm as well and refrain from trying to speed it up or distract them. **Let them get it out.**

When my son was around 2 years old, he had a tantrum that lasted about 45 minutes because he did not want to get dressed. He raged, he was angry, then he was sad, then he was embarrassed. He went through the full range of emotions. Gradually his cries slowed. He took a deep breath. "I'm ready to get dressed now." I stayed calm and our connection was maintained (and maybe even strengthened, because he knew I would love him even when he was upset).

If I had needed to leave quickly that day, I would have helped him get dressed using my hands as gently as possible and calmly applying the sportscasting technique mentioned earlier: "Are you having a hard time getting dressed? You can dress yourself, or I can help you. I see I'll need to help you. Yes, you are pulling your arm away. You don't want to put it in. I'm gently putting your T-shirt over your head. You are trying to push it off. Thanks for telling me that this is difficult."

Should I ignore a tantrum?

I have heard people suggest that it is better to ignore a tantrum completely. The idea is that helping children or giving attention to behavior we do not like or want means we are encouraging them.

I don't agree.

Imagine if I had a bad flight and told my friend that my luggage was lost, I was disappointed with the airline, and I hadn't gotten any help at all. If my friend ignored me and walked out of the room, I'd think they didn't care about me. I'd be angry with them because I had just wanted them to listen, help me calm down, or maybe ask if I'd like some space.

Ignoring the tantrum directs our child's feelings at us instead of at the problem that upset them. It creates a conflict just when they need connection.

Calm and kind acceptance encourages them to express their feelings. Over time, they will find healthier forms of expression, but they will not be scared to share their feelings with us because they will know that we are capable of being kind and calm even when they have feelings that are big and scary.

Setting up a calm space

In *Positive Discipline: The First Three Years*, Jane Nelsen talks about setting up a calm space for an older toddler around 3 years old, a place with some of their favorite things where they can go anytime they need to calm down. This is different from a time-out because the child can decide to go there and how long they would like to stay, and it is never used as a threat.

Instead, if we see them getting worked up, we can suggest it to them. "Would you like to go to your calm place to calm down?" or "Shall we go to your calm place together?" If they refuse and we want to calm ourselves down, we could say, "I think I'll go to the calm place myself." If they come out and are still fired up, we can kindly and calmly suggest that they might like to go back until they are feeling calmer.

The aim of this step is *not* to say that we accept their behavior. It's to help them first calm down.

RECONNECTING ONCE THEY ARE CALM

Once they are calm, they will be able to talk about what happened. We can offer a hug or wait for them to ask for one. We can then acknowledge their feelings and see things from their perspective. "Wow, was that difficult for you? You really didn't seem to like that. You looked furious."

HELPING THEM MAKE AMENDS

> "When everyone has calmed down, any damage should be addressed. Thrown items can be picked up, torn papers gathered and discarded, or pillows stacked back on the bed or sofa. Adults may offer to help a child with these tasks. It may also be appropriate to help your child repair additional damage, such as a broken toy . . . a very real way to learn about making things right."
>
> —Jane Nelsen, *Positive Discipline: The First Three Years*

Once our child has calmed down, we can help them make amends. This teaches them to take responsibility for their actions and is a very important step. Restorative justice ("How can we make this better?") is preferable to punishment (taking something away).

Yes, accept all their feelings (even the ugly ones) and help them calm down. Then once they are calm, we help them take responsibility for their behavior.

If we do this too soon before our toddler has calmed down, they will resist and will not want to make it better. That's why it is best to make sure they are calm first. Then they are really learning how to make it up to someone.

DEALING WITH TANTRUMS

UNDERSTAND TRIGGERS AND AVOID THEM IF POSSIBLE

- Frustration
- Anger or rage when things don't go their way
- Wanting to be in control
- Trouble communicating as their language may still be limited

HELP YOUR CHILD CALM DOWN

- Offer a cuddle—rub their back, hold them, sing to them as they go through the range of emotions, from anger to intense frustration to sadness and sometimes regret.
- If they push you away, make sure they are safe and not harming themselves, something, or someone. Stand nearby and keep offering help. "I'm here if you need some help calming down. Or we can have a cuddle when you are ready."
- If they are throwing toys at their sibling or trying to hit you, remove them so that everyone is safe. "I can't let you hit me. My safety is important to me. Would you like to hit these pillows instead?"

OLDER CHILDREN

- For a child over 3 years old, you can set up a "calm place" to use when they are upset, such as a tent with pillows and their favorite things or a corner with some trains.
- You can ask them if they would like to go to their calm place. If they come back still in a rage, we can gently tell them that they look like they still need to calm down and can come back when they are ready.

MAKING AMENDS—DON'T SKIP THIS STEP

Once they are calm, I help them make amends. For example, if they drew on the walls, they can help clean up; if they broke their brother's toy, they can help to fix it.

In this way, they learn to take responsibility when things go wrong.

How to make amends

If our child hit someone and they are calm again, we can help them see if the other child is okay, get a tissue for the other child, ask if they want to apologize, or some combination.

I often use an example from when my children were older to show how children can learn to make amends on their own over time. My daughter had a friend come to our house for a sleepover. My son was feeling a little left out and set the alarm in their room to go off at 4:00 a.m. When I heard them in the morning, my daughter and her friend were furious because the alarm had woken them up in the middle of the night. I stepped in to offer a little guidance, acknowledging both my son's feelings of being left out as well as the girls' anger at having been woken. In the end, they worked out that he would make them breakfast, and he was very pleased with himself as he cooked them French toast. Needless to say, when the same friend came for another sleepover, I asked him if he would wake them again. He was quick to say he wouldn't, and it hasn't happened again.

Modeling making amends

If they are still young, we can model it for them. "Let's go and see if our friend is okay." "I'm sorry my child hurt you. Are you feeling okay?" Modeling is more effective than forcing them to apologize if they don't mean it, having them mutter "Sorry" under their breath, or having them say it in a sarcastic tone.

We can model apologizing when we forget things, if we let people down, or if we bump into someone accidentally. We can model making amends to our child when we have regrets about how we have handled a conflict with them. As they grow, our child will learn to genuinely apologize.

For me, helping children to **take responsibility** when they have done something wrong is the most difficult part. Yet this is one of the most essential parts of helping these seeds grow into respectful human beings.

TIPS FOR SETTING LIMITS

Set limits early

It is difficult to be respectful to our children when we allow them to go beyond our limits. When we give too much. When we try to be accommodating and let them have too much freedom. We end up losing our temper and getting angry.

If we start to get uncomfortable about something our child is doing, we can step in early to set a kind and clear limit without losing our patience or shouting.

Or perhaps at first we feel okay with something they are doing but then notice we are starting to get irritated. It's not too late. We can say, "I'm sorry. I thought I was okay with you throwing the sand. I've changed my mind. I can't let you throw the sand." (If they become upset, see page 125 for tips on acknowledging negative feelings and dealing with tantrums.)

If we are getting upset

Remember that we are our child's guide. We cannot be a very good guide or leader when we get upset ourselves. They are looking to us for direction. If we are feeling upset by a difficult situation, it is likely that our toddler has a problem and is **making it our problem**. Our job is to support them while they are having a hard time. We do not need to fix it for them.

- When we are working really hard to get our child to eat dinner, they have made it our problem.
- When we are working really hard to get our child to get dressed, they have made it our problem.
- When we are working really hard to get our child to leave the playground, they have made it our problem.

Let them work it out—with our support.

- Provide nutritious meals for our child, but let them control how much they eat.
- Use a checklist to help set up a system with our child to get dressed, but take them out in their pajamas if they do not want to cooperate.
- Let them know we are leaving the playground in five minutes. Don't change the plan and stop to talk to another parent. Keep leaving the playground, helping them if needed.

Consistency

One last note on consistency. Toddlers are trying to make sense of the world around them. They will test limits to see if they are the same every day (often more than once a day). It really helps them when we know our limits. They learn that when we say "no," we mean "no." We are reliable, we are trustworthy, and we have their best interests in mind.

If we say "no" but then change our mind because they keep nagging and nagging, they will quickly learn that this works. This is what psychologists call *intermittent reinforcement*. If they get a different response one time, they will keep trying.

If we are not sure, we can say, "I'm not sure" or "Let's see."

Note: We can question why we say "no" in the first place. If we end up giving them the ice cream after they have nagged, perhaps we could have just said "yes" at the beginning and avoided being inconsistent.

TO PRACTICE

1. How can we cultivate cooperation with our child?
   - Is there a way to solve the problem with them?
   - Is there a way to give them a choice?
   - Is there a different way in which we could speak?
   - Do we need to manage our expectations or theirs?
   - Can we write a note?
2. When we set limits, are we kind and clear?
   - Do we have clear house/ground rules?
   - Is the child learning something?
3. Do we acknowledge their negative feelings to help them process their emotions?
4. Do we help them make amends once they have calmed down?

Children need parents who will show them they love them by:

- accepting them 100 percent for who they are
- giving them freedom to explore and be curious
- working with them to cultivate cooperation
- setting limits so that they are safe and learn to become respectful and responsible human beings

Let's be our child's guide. They don't need a boss or a servant.

> "The liberty of the child ought to have as its limits the collective interest of the community in which he moves; its form is expressed in what we call manners and good behaviour. It is our duty then to protect the child from doing anything which may offend or hurt others, and to check the behaviour which is unbecoming or impolite. But as regards all else, every action that has a useful purpose, whatever it may be and in whatever forms it shows itself, ought not only to be permitted, but it ought to be kept under observation; that is the essential point."
>
> —Dr. Maria Montessori, *The Discovery of the Child*

A HANDY CHECKLIST FOR LIMITS

IS THERE CLARITY?

- Have a few house rules.
- Be consistent with the limits.

IS THERE LOVE IN OUR LIMITS?

- Get down to their level.
- Use a clear and loving voice.
- Manage our own anger first.
- Give respect and understanding if they are sad or frustrated.
- Be there to hold them or keep them safe if they lose control.

IS THERE REASON BEHIND THE LIMIT?

- Is it connected to their safety or respect for others, their environment, or themselves?
- "Because I said so" is not a good enough reason.

IS THE LIMIT APPROPRIATE FOR THE CHILD'S AGE AND ABILITY?

- Limits can be revised as our child grows.

DOES IT INVITE CHILDREN TO FIND SOLUTIONS?

- Sometimes the best ideas are found by children themselves.

7

PUTTING IT INTO PRACTICE

PART ONE

DAILY CARE

I believe that we can take many of the daily struggles of life with a toddler and possibly even transform them into peaceful moments of connection. Did I mention I was an idealist?

DAILY RHYTHM

Toddlers thrive on regular rhythm. They like the predictability of knowing what is happening now and what is coming next. It provides them with a feeling of safety and security.

It does not have to be a fixed schedule kept to the exact minute. Rather, it can be valuable to have our rhythm follow the same pattern every day. The child is then able to predict what is coming next, which will minimize those difficult moments of transition. The rhythm follows the child's energy and interests. From time to time, it may well be different. We can then know ahead that this may be difficult for them and prepare ourselves (and our child) accordingly.

Moments of care = moments of connection

We spend a lot of our day caring for our toddler—helping them get dressed, eating meals together, changing diapers or helping them use the potty, and giving them a bath. Rather than seeing these daily care activities as something we need to get through quickly, we can see them as moments of connection with our child.

These can be times to smile, make eye contact, talk to them about what is happening, listen as they communicate (even if they do not yet have words), take turns in a conversation, show respectful ways to touch, and have hugs.

They present many opportunities to simply live together. And live together simply.

An example of a daily rhythm for a toddler

- Wake up
- Play in bedroom
- Cuddle with parent(s), read books
- Use potty/change diaper
- Breakfast
- Get dressed, wash face, and brush teeth
- Play at home/morning outing/visit market/leave for day care (if applicable)
- Lunch
- Use potty/change diaper
- Nap time/rest time
- Use potty/change diaper
- Play at home/afternoon outing
- Afternoon snack
- Get picked up from day care (if applicable)
- Play at home
- Dinner
- Bath
- Use potty/change diaper
- Story time
- Bedtime

RITUALS

Rituals in our family's life can be used to mark moments and establish memories.

At special moments during the year we may wish to make some rituals around events such as:

- birthdays
- holidays
- seasons—seasonal crafts, food, outings
- annual vacations
- regular weekly rituals like going to the park on Friday afternoons or making a special Sunday morning breakfast

Over time these rituals become familiar to our child, something to look forward to, and are often the things our children will remember the most from their childhood. Just as toddlers enjoy the predictability of daily rhythms, they love knowing what to expect around these events.

If the parents come from different backgrounds, cultures, and nationalities, it's an opportunity to come up with a unique way to celebrate these origins and create special new family traditions of our own.

Rituals may be created around the food we eat, the songs we sing, the people with whom we celebrate, or the things we make, like seasonal displays in our home.

In a Montessori school, we create a special celebration for each child's birthday. The child walks around a representation of the sun the same number of times as the number of years since their birth. This is a concrete way to show the passing of time and our relationship on earth to the sun.

As a child, I always knew exactly what food would be prepared for our backyard birthday parties and the party games we would play. Summer meant loads of mangoes and cherries, wearing swimsuits all day, and running around barefoot in the grass (and getting bindi-eyes—those horrible prickly weeds that grow in Australian grass—in my feet). I'm feeling surprisingly nostalgic now, even for the bindi-eyes.

At the end of the year here in Amsterdam, our family has many traditions. On the first of December, we make a homemade Advent calendar in which I hide little slips of paper with something fun to do each day, like going for a nighttime walk to see the festive lights, baking cookies, or making a craft. On December 5, we celebrate Sinterklaas with the Dutch tradition of writing poems and making surprises for each other. Later in the month during Hanukkah, we light some candles and sing "Maoz Tzur." And on Christmas Day, we exchange some presents and have a family meal. We keep each of these pretty low-key, inexpensive, and not too elaborate. The emphasis is on being together, rather than every moment having to be picture perfect.

For an in-depth look at some beautiful family rituals and traditions, I recommend reading *The Creative Family* by Amanda Blake Soule.

GETTING DRESSED AND LEAVING THE HOUSE

Getting dressed and leaving the house no longer have to be battles. Instead, we can apply the principles of guiding the child and finding ways to work with them, rather than threatening or bribing them.

Again, getting dressed can be used as a moment of connection—even if we are a parent who works outside the home.

Type of clothing

As our toddlers start trying to do things for themselves—"Me do it!"—look for easy clothing they can manage themselves or with little assistance.

Good choices:

- shorts and trousers with elastic waists that they can pull up without having to undo a zipper and/or button
- T-shirts with large openings for their head (or a press stud on the shoulder to open it wider)
- shoes with Velcro openings or buckles—easier than laces—or slip-on shoes

Avoid:

- long dresses, which can be difficult for toddlers to manage and restrict their movement
- overalls, which are difficult for the child to put on independently
- skinny jeans or other tight and restrictive clothing

A place for everything and everything in its place

As we explored in chapter 4, we can set up our homes in ways to make things easier for everyone. When we have a place for everything, then everything is (mostly) in its place and easy to find. We are less likely to be frantically searching for a missing glove or shoe.

For example, in the hallway, it is helpful to have:

- hooks for hanging coats and scarves
- a basket for gloves and hats
- a place for storing shoes
- a place to sit while putting on and removing shoes

With this preparation, the area is attractive and functional for getting out the door (and for when we get home, too). We'll have less "Where is the other shoe?" and more "Would you like to wear your black shoes or your blue shoes today?" Instead of a chaotic departure, it can be an opportunity to work together and create connection.

Learning to do it themselves

Don't forget that we can also take the time to teach children the skills for getting dressed when we are not in a hurry to leave the house. Toddlers love to be able to do things themselves. For example, we can teach them the Montessori coat flip so they can learn to put on their own coat.

The Montessori Coat Flip

1. Place the coat on the floor and have the child stand by the hood or label.
2. They place their hands in the sleeves and lift their arms up over their head.
3. The coat slides down and onto their body.

Scaffolding skills

Younger toddlers may need some help to get dressed. This is an opportunity to scaffold skills. They will learn how to dress if we break it down into small steps, each one building on the other, and over time will manage more and more of the process themselves.

Always observe to see how much help they need. Let them first try a step by themselves. Sit on our hands if we need to—it is so satisfying for them if they manage it successfully. We might put the T-shirt over their head and see if they can wiggle their arms into the sleeves.

When they are starting to get frustrated, we can offer some help. Step in to help a little and then step back to see how they manage. If they are stuck putting on their shoes, we may try holding the back of their shoe down while they put in their foot, and then see if they can succeed from there.

If they push us away completely, we can say, "Okay, just let me know if you need any help. I'm right here."

As our toddler gets older, they may be able to manage more and more steps independently. We might be able to get dressed at the same time in the same room. Or eventually we may find that we are able to leave the room and pop back to check on them now and again.

Slow down. Allow time. Connect.

How long does it take everyone in the house to get dressed when we don't need to leave the house? Maybe fifteen minutes? Twenty-five minutes? We can allow the same amount of time when we need to leave the house to get to school, work, or someplace else.

If we find it difficult to sit and watch a toddler get dressed at toddler pace, we can find a way to make the process enjoyable, like bringing in a cup of tea or coffee (keep hot drinks out of their reach) or putting on some relaxing or upbeat music.

When they don't want to get dressed

Be prepared for times when they won't want to dress themselves. It can be frustrating to see our child refuse to put their own shoe on when it seemed just yesterday they were pleased to have accomplished it on their own. Remember, we don't want to cook dinner every day either. Be prepared to help, perhaps offering, "Would you like some help with your shoe today?"

Remember that toddlers are in the process of becoming independent from us—some days they will want us to help and sometimes they will want to do it themselves. It's what I like to call *the crisis of independence.*

If it is an ongoing problem, we can go back and review the ideas on working with our child to encourage cooperation in chapter 6. Here are some ideas that would be useful for getting dressed:

- waiting until they have finished their activity
- allowing them time to process our requests
- offering them choices of clothing
- using humor
- keeping our expectations age appropriate
- using a checklist

Note: If they don't want to have their diaper changed, it may be because they don't like to lie on their backs while it's happening. It can feel like a very vulnerable position. Although it is more convenient for us if they lie down, with some practice we can sit on a low stool to change them while the child stands between our knees. For bowel movements, we can get the child to lean forward and hold onto the edge of the bathtub or a low stool while we clean their bottom.

When we need to leave

Even though we can allow children time to go slowly, we don't have to be saints and allow unlimited amounts of time. If we run out of time, we can say something like, "You really want to get dressed by yourself, and it is time to leave. I'm going to help you put the last things on." Know our boundaries and set a limit when needed.

Use our gentle hands and sportscast to help acknowledge any resistance they are giving. "I am putting on your T-shirt. Yes, you are pulling away. Are you trying to tell me you don't like it when it goes over your head? Now I'm going to help you with your left arm . . ."

You can also go stand by the front door. Instead of saying, "I'm leaving without you," we could say calmly and clearly, "I'm not leaving without you. I'm putting on my shoes now and will be by the front door."

EATING

Mealtimes are another moment for connection—for our toddlers to learn that meals are social occasions, as well as times for nourishing our bodies.

There can be a lot of stress around mealtimes. As parents, we want to make sure our toddlers eat enough to stay healthy and maybe so they will not wake up hungry at nighttime. We may have gotten into the habit of letting them walk around with a snack or feeding them as they play so we know they have eaten. Sometimes it's the other way around, and we are worried our toddler is eating too much.

A Montessori approach to eating is quite different. We create a beautiful setting, maybe with a few flowers on the table. The child can help us prepare the meal and set the table (with help at first), and as often as possible, we sit down together for a family meal.

The adult's role

We are laying the foundations for our child's relationship with food and for good eating habits. The adult decides where, when, and what the child will eat. Rather than the parent feeding the toddler, we set things up so the child can successfully feed themselves and choose how much they want to eat at their own pace. No flying airplanes, bribes with dessert, or using the television or iPad to distract them.

Setting a rule like sitting at the table for meals helps our children learn the following:

- meals are social occasions and a time for connection
- sitting at the table is safer than walking around with food in their mouth
- we do one thing at a time (eat or play, not both)
- food stays at the table

As we discussed in chapter 4, we can set up our kitchen so the child can be independent, as well as be involved in the meal preparation. Children often have more interest in food when they are involved with preparing the meal, and they can learn to get a drink when needed if they can reach a water source by themselves.

Where—a place to eat

I know that children often eat early in the evening and that our evening schedules can feel rushed when combining work and children. However, we are the best model for them to learn manners and to learn that mealtimes are social occasions. So it can be great to sit down to have meals together with our child. If we do not want to eat a full meal so early, we could have something small, like a bowl of soup.

Personally I like eating main meals at the family dining/kitchen table. So it is useful to find a seat that the child can get in and out of independently rather than high chairs with straps and a tray table in front, which keeps them farther from the table and requires our assistance.

We can also have a low table where the child sits on a low chair with their feet flat on the floor. I like to use this at snack time, sitting on a low chair or a floor cushion to join them. I know some people use this for all meals. It's up to each family.

I would not expect toddlers to sit at the table until everyone finishes their meal. In our house, when they were all finished, they would take their plate to the kitchen and go play. As they got older, they would gradually stay longer at the table to enjoy the conversation.

If they walk away from the table with food or a fork in their hand, we can say: "I'll keep the food/fork at the table. It's okay for you to go." I say this a lot in my classes when children are learning to sit at our snack table. If they want to keep eating, they sit back down with the food. If not, I model clearing things away to show that by leaving, they are choosing to be all finished.

When—time to eat

Keeping with the daily rhythm discussed earlier, I like to offer meals at regular times during the day—rather than having the kitchen open at all hours. Three meals a day (breakfast, lunch, dinner) and a small snack in the morning and/or afternoon. This gives time for their bodies to digest food and helps them refrain from filling up too much on snack foods.

What—type of foods to eat

As the adult, we can decide what food we would like our family to eat. If we want to offer a choice, we could offer the child two options that we find acceptable. They are not yet capable of making good food choices completely by themselves but will learn about these choices by the food we offer and the conversations we have.

From 12 months, a toddler no longer needs a bottle to drink and can take regular milk in a glass at mealtimes. Start with a small amount in a small glass, filled only as full as we are prepared to clean up. Over time, they will master the skill and have no need for a sippy cup or bottle. We may also be offering breastfeeding, usually at regular moments in the day.

My children were allowed some sugar now and then, applying an "everything in moderation" approach. They still eat sugar occasionally but are remarkably self-disciplined. Again this is a personal decision—just be consistent.

How much—the child's choice

Fortunately, the days of being told to finish everything on our plates are long gone. We want our children to learn to listen to their bodies to understand when they are full. Rather than filling up a toddler's plate (which can feel overwhelming or end up on the floor), we can start with a small amount of food and let them serve themselves more if they would like.

Leave the child in charge. Trust that they are taking enough. Children at this age generally will not starve themselves. They will take as much as they need if we remove our control around food and trust them to listen to their bodies.

If our child is not a big eater, we will often observe that their appetite fluctuates. Sometimes they don't seem to finish anything on their plate, yet during growth spurts, they may eat three meals a day, plus snacks, and still be hungry. Their bodies know exactly what they need.

A young toddler can also learn to use cutlery to feed themselves. A fork is easier to use than a spoon at the beginning. We can show them how to pierce a piece of food with the fork, and leave it in front of them so they can bring it to their own mouth. Then they will take over more and more steps themselves. For learning to use a spoon, we can provide thicker offerings like oatmeal until they gain more mastery.

Food battles

If we find ourselves needing to hand-feed our child, bribe them, or distract them with books or TV to get them to eat, then they are making mealtimes our problem. It's time to reestablish good eating habits.

We can explain simply to our child that we have changed our mind about mealtimes. We can tell them that we want to enjoy our food together and it is important that they learn to listen to their own body to decide how much they will eat for themselves.

Start at breakfast time. Offer a nutritious breakfast, and then sit down with them and eat breakfast, too, talking about anything (except food!). If they do not eat anything, simply ask if they are finished (no lecturing) and help them bring their plate to the kitchen. We could say, "You listened to your body, and it said it was all done."

If they come back asking for food, we can be understanding but clear that the meal is all finished and there will be more food at the next meal.

Repeat at lunchtime and dinner. It's a good idea to avoid snacks for a few days so they don't fill up on them while we are trying to improve mealtimes. If they have not eaten very much, likely by the end of the day they will be hungry and eat some food at dinner. Include some of their favorite foods, but don't make different food if they demand it. They are also learning to eat what the family is eating.

Continue this for one week and keep a diary of what the child eats. Write it down, stick the list on the fridge, and be unattached to the outcome. Don't make a big deal about food or mention it much at all. Have confidence. It may take only a few days before the food battles have been replaced by a child who sits at the table and feeds themselves.

Note: Make sure the child doesn't have any medical reasons for refusing to eat or have other food-related issues. If there is no improvement in eating after a week or if you have any concerns, consult a doctor. There may also be a change in the child's bowel movements as their digestion adjusts.

Throwing food

Toddlers like to explore the world around them. Throwing food off their plate can be an experiment to see what happens when it falls. Usually they start throwing their food when they have had enough to eat: **They are telling us they are all finished**. We can ask them, "Are you telling me you are all finished?" We can show them a sign with both our hands out, palms up. "You can say 'all finished' like this. All finished. Now let's take our plates to the kitchen. Let me know if you need some help."

If they are not finished eating but continue to throw their food, we can be **kind and clear** and tell them that we will help them take the plate to the kitchen. Again not with a threatening tone, simply setting a clear limit. Generally food throwing is a phase. Remain calm and (yes) consistent. It will pass.

Similarly if they were spilling their water on purpose, I would take their glass away. "I'm going to put the glass over here. Let me know when you would like to use the glass for drinking." If they asked for it but then poured it on the table again, I would calmly remove it for the rest of the meal.

SLEEPING

We can apply Montessori principles when it comes to sleeping—whether we choose to have our child in their own room, in their own bed in our room, or co-sleeping in a family bed. In our Montessori training, they recommended having the child in their own room, but sleeping is a very personal choice, so find an arrangement that works best for the family.

Around 12 to 16 months, a toddler will generally move to one nap time in the middle of the day and then sleep at night from ten to twelve hours. If our child is getting more or less than this, we will know if our child is getting enough sleep if they generally wake happy and are pretty happy during the day.

Where to sleep

A toddler's sleeping place should be truly restful. Make the sleeping area safe and free from too many distractions and visual clutter. Look for a way for the child to be able to get into and out of bed independently. By around 14 months, they could move into a toddler bed with a low side that they are able to climb into independently, or use a floor mattress.

We may wish to use a night-light. In Sarah Ockwell-Smith's article "One Simple Way to Improve Your Baby or Child's Sleep Today!" she advises avoiding white- and blue-based lights and looking for red-based light, which does not affect melatonin production.

We can have a drink at the ready if children are thirsty in the night.

We also may choose a family bed or allow our children to come in during the night. It is up to each family.

Just be clear on what is okay. If we are complaining about a toddler's sleep, it's likely that a part of the sleeping arrangement is not working for us, and we may need to make a change.

Getting to sleep

I have shared a lot about the importance of giving the child just as much help as they need. We support them, step in to help, and step back again. The same goes for sleep.

Establish a clear, regular bedtime sequence. Allow around an hour to have a bath, brush teeth, read some books, and talk about all the things that happened that day. Then give only as much help as they need to fall asleep.

Some children have a good relationship with sleep from birth and will simply put themselves to bed when they are tired (often on a floor mattress, from birth)—the holy grail. These children often have clear sleep associations from birth, and consistent bedtime sequences. They go to bed drowsy but awake, do not have sleep crutches, and feed separately from falling asleep.

Some toddlers may be happy to read books and fall asleep by themselves, whereas others may need to cry at bedtime. If we know they have eaten well, have a dry diaper, and have had a good play, then their crying is saying they are ready to sleep. But I would not recommend leaving them to cry it out alone.

A nice, gentle technique to help them fall asleep by themselves is to place a chair by their bed. Once the bedtime sequence is finished, sit in the chair quietly (maybe read a book). If they are crying, rub their back occasionally and say something soothing, rather than picking them up. We can lay them back down if they stand up and not engage in conversation or too much eye contact.

Once they have learned to fall asleep like this, we can move our chair farther away from the bed and repeat for a few nights. Every few nights the chair moves closer to the door, and after about two weeks, we can sit in the chair outside the door where they can still see us. After a couple of nights, the child usually no longer needs us to sit with them.

If they are sick or teething, they may need some additional support from us. These things can disrupt their sleeping pattern, and we will need to reestablish it once they are feeling better.

Sleep crutches and night waking

We all drift in and out of light sleep during the night, move around a little, and then resettle. Generally we resettle so quickly, we don't remember waking. If the conditions change, however—for example, if our pillow has fallen off the bed—we will wake up, look around until we find it, and then need to get back to sleep.

The same is true with babies and toddlers. If they fall asleep while being rocked or fed, they will wake up from light sleep during their nap or night sleep and look for the adult, unable to resettle until the same conditions are established. We become their sleep crutch.

I got into a crazy cycle with my firstborn. I rocked him to sleep for months, he often fed to sleep, and he'd wake often at night looking for the breast. I'd feed him again, his tummy would hurt (in hindsight, I realize that he probably hadn't had time to digest his food), and he'd wake again.

I learned my lesson. With my second child, we kept a clear daily rhythm from birth. Eat, play, sleep. It was much clearer for us (and her) when it was time to rest. She lay in bed drowsy but awake before falling asleep, loved sleeping in her bed, and needed very little help at all to sleep (though she wouldn't sleep while out and about—probably too much to see).

Learn from my mistakes and remove sleep crutches.

If the child is waking to be fed at night and we want to remove the sleep crutch of feeding to sleep, we can look for ways to feed less during the night. Watering down the milk gradually in a bottle is an option. I know one breastfeeding mother who fell asleep by accident on the couch one night. Asleep in the other room, their child didn't wake up. So she slept on the couch in the living room for a week and their child stopped waking to feed.

If they are waking at night to request a cuddle or a drink, to have their cover adjusted, or to find their favorite soft toys, I would discuss those things during the day, at a neutral time. "You know how you woke up last night and couldn't get back to sleep without your covers over you? Let's think of a way that you can take care of it yourself in the night. Do you have any ideas? Perhaps we can put the cover across the bed and tuck it in extra tight, or practice pulling up the covers."

If a child is continuing to have sleep difficulties that **affect the well-being of the child or the family**, please see a sleep specialist.

BRUSHING TEETH

There are no official Montessori guidelines for brushing teeth, but it is a commonly asked question when children do not like brushing their teeth.

We come back to having a respectful relationship with the toddler. We are working with our children, where they are today. We let them lead. They choose whether to brush their teeth before, during, or after their bath. They come with us to the store to select the toothbrush they want. But we are clear that teeth brushing is not optional.

Again, we set things up for the child to be independent so they can help themselves. For a toddler, that might mean helping them at the end to "finish off" and make sure their teeth are clean. When we assist, we do so gently and respectfully. It must feel pretty strange for someone to poke a toothbrush in our mouth if we are a toddler.

We could brush our teeth alongside our child to help give them a concrete understanding of caring for our teeth. We can sing, "This is the way we brush our teeth, brush our teeth, brush our teeth. This is the way we brush our teeth every night and morning." Not to distract them, just to make it a light moment in our day.

If our child detects that we are trying to distract them, they may feel like we are tricking them rather than getting their cooperation and may resist even more. Just as stickers work for a while as a reward, distraction works only up to a point before they tire of that "trick" and you need to work even harder to keep them on task.

If we have tried working with them and they are still avoiding brushing their teeth, we can say calmly with confidence and handling them very gently, "Now I'm going to help you brush your teeth. We are going back to the bathroom. I'm opening your mouth . . ." We are being kind and clear.

PART TWO

DEALING WITH CHANGES

TOILETING

The period when a toddler learns how to use the toilet does not have to be dreaded. After all, it is a completely natural part of being a human. Our children pick up our attitudes toward dirty diapers from infancy, and if we are screwing up our face, they will learn that it is a dirty thing instead of a normal bodily process.

I love this analogy from a fellow Montessori teacher. When a baby pulls themselves up to standing, falls down, stands up again, and then falls down, over and over until they master it, we think it is cute. When our child is learning to use the bathroom and they pee on the floor or poop in their pants, they are also practicing until they master it—except there is pee and poop.

So with open minds, I would love to help make this process a little less stressful.

Scaffolding skills

The child will slowly build skills around using the toilet, starting with being able to manage their own clothing. At first they practice pulling their shorts or trousers up and down, and then later their underwear.

We can offer a potty/toilet when we change their diaper, never forcing them, but making it part of the daily rhythm. "Would you like to sit on the potty/toilet?" "Now that you're finished on the potty, I'm going to put your diaper back on."

Using cloth diapers can also help the child feel wet when they have peed, increasing their body awareness.

Signs of readiness—Let the child lead

The most important thing is to follow our child. It is not a competition.

I'm not including any ages here, but rather, signs that the child may be ready:

- pulling at their diaper when it is wet or soiled
- squatting or going to a private place while they poop
- telling us they have peed or pooped
- resisting having their diaper changed (sometimes)
- taking off their diaper

Set up the bathroom with our child

Have a potty or a small toilet seat on the toilet. If they are using the toilet, we will need a step that the child can manage themselves and as a place to rest their feet to feel secure while sitting on the toilet.

We can also have a place in the bathroom for soiled clothes and a pile of clean underwear. A pile of cleaning rags for puddles is useful, too.

Having everything at the ready and being prepared will help us remain relaxed and not rushing about, looking for things. If they don't make it to the potty/toilet, we can calmly say, "Ah. I see you are wet. We have everything we need right here. Let's get dry."

Keep it normal

Involve the child in the process. Buy some underwear together, as well as a potty. We can also find training pants that hold a little bit of pee to help when they are trying to get to the toilet in time.

As we are scaffolding skills, we can start by letting them wear just their underpants when we are at home so there is less to have to take on and off, and less to wash. They are learning what it feels like to be wet and may even stand to watch the pee run down their leg. That's the first step. Increasing body awareness.

Next we can help them go to the bathroom to change. Montessori teachers generally say, "You have wet clothes. Let's go change," rather than, "You had an accident."

Offer the potty/toilet regularly at first. If we ask a toddler if they need to go to the toilet, they usually answer "no." It's a common response for a toddler who is developing autonomy. Instead, we can wait until they aren't in the middle of an activity and simply say, "It's time to go to the potty," leading them to the bathroom.

After some weeks, they generally will begin to have more awareness of their body and sometimes tell us that they need to go to the toilet. We will also observe that they are able to hold it in for longer periods at a time. Eventually they won't need reminders at all.

Dry at night

We can move to underpants at nap time and night at the same time or when we notice they can hold for longer periods and wake with a dry diaper/underwear.

Place a thick towel across the child's sheets and tuck it in, or use a bed protector; either can easily be removed during the night if needed.

Holding it in

Sometimes a child becomes scared of pooping. It may have hurt once to poop, someone may have had a reaction that made them scared to poop on the toilet, or we may not know why. Check with a doctor if you believe there is a medical issue.

If all appears healthy, help the child relax by being calm and supportive. We can tell them, "The poop will come out when it is ready. It may take a week, it may take two weeks, but it knows when to come. Our bodies are very clever." Then try not to talk about it too much. Rub their tummy if their abdomen hurts.

If they usually go somewhere private to poop, gradually invite the child to move to the bathroom to poop in private. Then we can start to invite them to sit on the potty with their diaper on. Gradually they will feel safe on the potty/toilet without the diaper/ underwear on. Again, we are simply supporting them and scaffolding skills.

If they refuse to use the toilet

We don't force a child to use the toilet. This is their body. We can't rush it or do this for them. We can only support them and find ways to work with them.

We can make sure we aren't interrupting them to take them to the bathroom. We can keep offering the potty/toilet and trust that they will learn to use them. We accept them for who they are and where they are in this process.

Peeing on the floor intentionally

Sometimes a toddler who knows how to use the toilet will suddenly start to pee on the floor intentionally. Observe them. Often they are telling us through their behavior that they are unhappy about something in their world, for example, a sibling who has started crawling and taking more of their space.

They want us to see them, and we can look from a place of curiosity, in order to understand them. We can acknowledge their feelings but set a clear limit about the behavior. "You're upset about something? I can't let you pee on the floor. But I want to work it out with you." We can go back to creating connection, finding ways to work with them, and do some problem solving together with them. (See chapters 5 and 6.)

SAYING GOODBYE TO PACIFIERS

When applying the Montessori approach, pacifiers aren't used much or are phased out within the first year. If a young toddler still uses a pacifier, phasing them out does not have to be a difficult process.

Even though the child is young, we can let them know that we are going to make a change.

The first step is to start using the pacifier only for sleeping. When our child wakes, we can put it in a box by the bed out of reach, so our child (or even the adult) will not be tempted to use it.

If our child asks for the pacifier at other times, we can try to observe why they feel the need to suck and address the root cause. Maybe they need something engaging to do with their hands or a toy to play with, maybe they are seeking connection and we can offer a cuddle, or maybe they need help to calm down or to relax their nervous system.

Here are some ideas that may help:

- sucking yogurt through a straw
- blowing bubbles
- holding tightly on to a book or soft toy
- using a bottle with a straw
- blowing water through a straw to make bubbles
- a brisk towel rub after a bath
- deep-pressure bear hugs
- kneading dough
- squeezing bath toys
- a slow, firm back rub

We can then make a plan with our toddler to get rid of the pacifier at bedtime, too. One popular choice is to give it to a friend with a new baby.

It generally takes a few days for the child to learn to fall asleep without it, during which they may need a little—just enough—extra support. Be careful not to add any new sleeping crutches into the routine. (For children who find this difficult in the middle of the night, see the section on sleeping, beginning on page 147.)

SIBLINGS

Often parents tell me that these ideas would be simple to carry out if they had only one child. Having more than one child makes it difficult for parents to find time to observe each child, meet their individual needs, and deal with arguments among siblings. Not to mention that having a new baby in the home, or an older sibling bossing them around, can be disruptive to a toddler.

The new baby

In their book *Siblings Without Rivalry*, Adele Faber and Elaine Mazlish open with a story that illustrates the effect a new sibling can have on a child's life.

Imagine that our partner comes home one day and says that they love us so much, they are going to get another partner, in addition to us. The new partner is going to sleep in our old bed and use our clothes, and we are going to share everything with them. I think many of us would be furious and feel very jealous. So it's not surprising that a new addition to the family can have a huge effect on some children.

We can do a lot to prepare our toddler before the baby arrives. We can talk to our child about what life with a new baby might look like. Especially helpful are books with realistic pictures showing parents looking after the baby while still spending time with the other children in the home. We can let them talk and sing to the baby in the belly and begin to build a connection. We can let them help prepare the baby's space. And we can make a point of enjoying our last days together in our current family configuration. (The memory of going to the park with my son the day before my daughter was born is one I'll always cherish.)

When it's time to introduce our toddler to the new baby (if our toddler has not been present at the birth), we can put down the baby before they enter the room so our attention is solely on them. This can be easier for the toddler than walking in to see us holding the new baby in our arms.

Try to keep the early weeks at home simple and, if possible, have extra hands to help. We can ask others to help with the newborn for some of the time, so we can have time to be alone with our toddler.

Some toddlers like to be involved in caring for the new baby—fetching a clean diaper or getting soap for the baby's bath. Some won't be interested, and that's okay, too.

We can keep a basket of books and some favorite toys on hand while we feed, so we can feed the baby and connect with our toddler at the same time.

When the toddler is playing and the baby is awake, it can be fun to talk to the baby about what the toddler is doing. The baby will benefit from our conversation, and the toddler will like being the topic of discussion.

(For ideas on how to set up the home with more than one child, see page 75.)

When the toddler gets upset about the new baby

Our toddler may say they hate the new baby. They may be emotional or difficult or intentionally destructive at this disruptive time in their life.

This behavior is simply their way of telling us they are having a hard time. Instead of saying, "You don't really hate the baby," and denying their feelings, remember that they need us to see things from their perspective, to be understanding and to offer them connection.

We can allow all the angry feelings. We can ask, "Is it annoying you that they are touching the one thing you are playing with?" and listen to them. Really allow them to let it out.

But we don't have to allow all behavior. For example, if they are hitting the baby, here are some things we can do:

- Step in immediately and remove their hands gently. "I can't let you hit the baby. We are gentle with the baby."
- We can translate for the baby. "The baby is crying. They are saying that's too much."
- We can show them a safer way to interact. "Let's show the baby this soft toy instead."

Make special time with each child

We can find creative ways to spend regular one-on-one time with our toddler: a trip to the supermarket, a walk down the road to a cafe for a snack, or a visit to the playground for ten minutes on the swing.

Then, when they want something from us and we're not available, we can write it down in a notebook and talk about it during our special time together.

Stay neutral

Siblings like to draw us into their disputes to take sides. My favorite advice (which I need to remind myself of at times) is to stay neutral and not take sides in these conflicts.

Our role is to **support both children**, keep them safe if needed, and help mediate so that both parties take responsibility. We see things from both perspectives and give them just as much help as they need.

Yes, even with a toddler. There was a time when my children were young (2 years old and 9 months old) and both wanted the same toy truck. It's tempting to solve the problem for them—find another toy, distract one of them, try to get them to share. However, I simply said, "One truck and two children. Now, that's a problem." Then my son took off the back part of the truck and gave it to his sister, keeping the front wheels for himself. He thought of something far more creative than I would have come up with.

Parent as if we have a big family

In his book *Thriving!* parenting educator Michael Grose suggests that we raise siblings as if we have a large family with four or more children. Parents of large families can't solve every argument and entertain every child. Parents are the leaders of the family. They lay the foundations of the family's values and oversee the running of the ship.

When to step in

Generally when children fight, we rush in and ask, "Who did it?" The children immediately try to defend themselves or blame their sibling: "They started it!"

Here are alternative ways to step in if siblings are fighting.

1. Be visible

During minor arguments, we can let them see that we are in the room and then leave again. Think of this as an important experience in conflict resolution. They know that we have seen them arguing, but we are confident they can work it out themselves.

2. Observe

When arguing heats up, we can stay and observe. They will feel our presence without our having to say anything.

3. Remind them of the house/ground rules

We may need to remind them of a rule. For example, if it sounds like rough play is going too far, we can check in with them. We can say, "Rough play by mutual consent" or "Do you need to say stop? You don't sound like you are having fun anymore."

4. Provide some support

When they can't work it out themselves, we can give them support to help them solve the conflict:

- Listen to both sides (without judgment).
- Acknowledge how both parties feel, and show that we understand and can see things from both of their perspectives.
- Describe the problem.
- Express interest in hearing how they work it out.
- Move away to let them find a solution.

An example:

"You two sound mad at each other." (Acknowledge their feelings.)

"So Sara, you want to keep holding the puppy. And you, Billy, want to have a turn too." (Reflect each child's point of view.)

"That's a tough one: two children and one puppy." (Describe the problem.)

"I have confidence that you two can work out a solution that's fair to each of you . . . and fair to the puppy." (Move away.)

5. Separate children so they can calm down

When we start to feel uncomfortable with the level of fighting, we can step in to separate them. "I see two angry children. I can't let you hurt each other. You go over here, and you go over there until everyone is calm."

Even with preverbal children, it's the same process.

6. Problem solve

Once the fighting has calmed down, we can do some problem solving together. As we discussed in chapter 6:

- Everyone brainstorms ideas of how to solve the problem (with younger toddlers, we might come up with most of the ideas).
- We decide upon a solution that everyone can live with.
- We follow up to see if the solution is working or needs to be adjusted.

Foster gratitude for, and positive interactions with, siblings

Generally, the more we foster positive interactions between our children, the closer they become. We can create situations for them to enjoy each other's company, regardless of whether there is a large age gap.

At neutral times, we can discuss the positive side of having siblings or ask our children what they like about having a sibling.

Even if they aren't close friends, we can expect them to treat each other with respect.

Treating each child individually

Just as counting out an equal number of peas at every meal is nearly impossible, so is trying to parent our children equally. Instead, we can strive to parent our children **individually, based on their needs**.

There will be times when one child needs more one-on-one time from us, perhaps around their birthday or when passing through a developmental change. Each sibling learns that we will be available when they need our help.

If the children demand our attention at the same time, we can say, "As soon as I have finished here, I will come help you." And if two children want to speak at the same time, we can let them know that we are available to listen to both of them, although not at the same time. "First I'll finish listening to you [Child A], and then I really want to hear what you [Child B] have to say."

We can also avoid comparing siblings. It is easy to make offhand comments like "Look at your brother eating his dinner."

Children themselves may try to compete with their siblings. Again, we can bring the focus back to the individual, rather than making it about their sibling. For example, if one child says that their sibling has more cheese, we can say, "Did you want more cheese?" thereby treating each child individually.

Labels

For more on avoiding labels and accepting each sibling for who they are, see chapter 5.

PART THREE

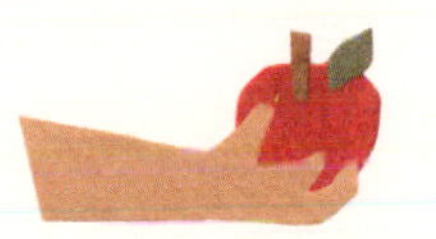

USEFUL SKILLS FOR OUR TODDLERS TO LEARN

SHARING

When our child was a baby, they may have easily handed things to us or, when something was taken out of their hand, they may have simply turned around to find something else to play with.

This willingness to share changes when they become a toddler, as they develop a heightened sense of "I," and want to practice something until mastery. Suddenly, around 14 to 16 months, we may see them pull their activity close to them, push away another child who is watching them at work, or shout "No!" to an innocent toddler walking by.

Before 2.5 years, toddlers are mostly interested in parallel play—playing on their own alongside another child—rather than sharing their toys and playing together. So we may need to adjust our expectations that a toddler will be able to share their toys. (If they have older siblings or play regularly with others in day care, they may learn to share a little earlier.)

Share by taking turns

Instead of asking the child to share their activity with someone else, in Montessori schools the ground rule is that we share by taking turns. We have only one of each activity; a child can work as long as they like with it (to allow repetition, concentration, and mastery); and children learn to wait their turn, a useful skill.

We can have the same rule in our home and provide support if needed:

- Observe to see if they are happy to allow another child to watch or join in the activity. We can see a lot from their body language, and give only as much help as they need. Allow them to resolve low-level disputes as much as possible by themselves.
- Help them use words if someone wants their toy. "My turn. It will be available soon." They can put their hands on their hips for emphasis.

- Help the child who is having trouble waiting. "Do you want a turn right now? It will be available soon."
- If a child is being physical, we can step in to be a bodyguard, maybe by using a gentle hand or placing our body between the children. "I can't let you push them. Are you telling them that you were playing with that?"

Around 2.5 years, they may become interested in playing with another child for a while. They may need some guidance, for example, to help them with some words or to learn from situations that come up. "It looks like Peter wants to play by himself now. Let's come back later and you can have a turn then."

At the playground or in public places

It can be difficult in public places where different families have different rules.

If someone is waiting for our child to finish on the swing, we can say to the other child, "It looks like you'd like a turn. You can have a turn when our child is all finished. The swing will be available very soon." Then they (and their parent) know that we see they would like a turn and they will be next.

To our child, we could say, "I see another child is waiting to use the swing. Let's count to ten and then we'll give them a turn." Rather than staying with the activity until our child is completely finished, we are modeling grace and courtesy toward others.

Sharing with visitors

When visitors are coming over, we can ask our children if there are any toys they would like to put away in a cupboard. Then we can check that they are happy for the visitors to play with everything else. We are helping them prepare themselves and have a say in what their friends can play with.

LEARNING HOW TO INTERRUPT AN ADULT

Although Montessori is a child-led approach to education, a young child can learn to wait and interrupt conversations in a respectful way.

My children's first Montessori teacher told the children that if she was in the middle of giving a lesson to another child and they had something they needed to tell her, they should put their hand on her shoulder. This would tell her that they had something important to say. Then, as soon as there was an appropriate place to pause in the lesson, she would stop and see what the child needed.

This principle can be used in the home, too. If we are on a phone call or talking to someone and our toddler has something to say, we can tap our shoulder to remind them to put their hand there. They place their hand there, and as soon as we can, we ask them what they wanted to say.

It takes practice, but it really works. A hand on our shoulder, with our hand on theirs, gives them the message, "What you have to tell me is important. I'll be right with you."

SKILLS FOR INTROVERTED TODDLERS

Parents of more introverted children may be worried that their child is not as confident or outgoing as other children. Or they may recognize that their child is an introvert, but worry that they don't have the skills to manage in a world that expects a child to maneuver confidently through social situations.

In her book *Quiet: The Power of Introverts in a World That Can't Stop Talking*, Susan Cain argues that introverts are undervalued for their empathy and their ability to listen. As parents of introverts, we can help support them without trying to change them.

First of all **accept them for who they are**. Jump back to chapter 5 for a refresher on these principles. Avoid using labels like *shy*. These can become crutches, excusing a child from awkward situations ("They're just shy"). Instead, we can help them learn how to manage these situations ("Do you want some more time to warm up/join in?"). And try not to compare them to siblings or other children by saying things like, "Look how well they play with the others."

Then, from this place of acceptance, we can **see things from their perspective and offer understanding. Acknowledge their feelings**. We can listen to them or hold them if needed. "Are you feeling worried about going to Grandma's house/the birthday party/the supermarket?" Allow them to feel safe.

It can help to **prepare them in advance** for situations that might make them nervous by giving them an idea of what to expect.

If our child takes some **time to warm up** in social situations, allow them to stand by us and observe the scene until they are ready to join in. We don't need to give them any special attention or make it a big deal. We can carry on our adult conversation; the child will drift off once they are ready.

Over time, we can help our child **build skills** that will empower them, so that they don't feel like they cannot handle certain situations.

Such skill building could include:

- Role playing. For example, they can practice saying "hello" to the adult at the door and "happy birthday" to the child having the party.
- Showing them how to excuse themselves to have a break, if they are finding a social situation overwhelming. For example, "I'm just going to have some quiet time."
- Practicing in less confrontational situations, such as handing over the money in a shop or ordering a drink in a cafe. We will be there to support them if needed. "Would you be able to say that a little louder? It looks like the waiter can't hear you."
- Practicing easy phrases they can use to be assertive. For example, "Stop. I don't like that."
- Showing them how to use their body language, such as putting their hands on their hips if someone has done something they don't like.

Finally, we can help them **gain confidence** by celebrating the skills they do have and by learning how to care for themselves, others, and the environment.

On the other hand, if our child is very confident and loves to run up to other children and hug them, we can translate for the child who does not seem to be enjoying their attention. "It looks like they are pulling away. Maybe we should check to see if they feel like being hugged." Our child may take it personally that the other child isn't as excited as they are; we can model how to accept other children the way they are.

As adults, it is also useful to remember to check in with any child before we handle them, particularly if they are not our child. We can check with them before we give them a hug ("Would you like a hug?" rather than "Give me a hug!"), tell a young toddler we are going to pick them up and get their consent before handling them, and ask if they'd like help before we do something for them. We respect that the child has a say about if, when, and how they will be handled.

A HITTING/BITING/PUSHING/ THROWING PHASE

Toddlers are learning how to communicate. Sometimes they use words or sounds. Sometimes they use body language. And sometimes they hit, bite, or push us or other children. It is another way of communicating. It isn't desirable, but it is a phase we can support and help them through.

First, let me say that if our child is hitting, biting, or pushing other children, we should be prepared to shadow our child in social situations and be ready to step in to keep other children safe. We don't have to be anxious—our child will pick up on it—but we can stay close or sit on the ground next to them to support them. We can step in gently or place a hand between the children if needed. We can acknowledge their feelings while stopping the behavior and separating the children.

We may also want to limit outings that are likely to make our child uncomfortable and trigger this behavior (lots of children, a noisy environment, etc.), at least for a time.

Observing the behavior

A Montessori teacher's answer to almost everything is to first observe. We are looking to see what kind of situations seem to cause the behavior. Here are some questions we can ask:

- **Time.** What time does the behavior happen? Is our child hungry or tired?
- **Changes.** Are they teething? Are there any changes at home, such as a new baby or a new house?
- **Activity.** What are they doing/playing with at the time of being triggered?
- **Other children.** How many children are around? Are the children the same age, younger, or older?
- **Emotion being expressed.** Just before it happens, how do they look? Playful? Frustrated? Confused?
- **Environment.** Look at the environment where it happens. Is it busy? Is it very colorful or otherwise too stimulating? Is there a lot of clutter? Is there a lot of children's artwork around the room, which is possibly too much sensory input? Or is it peaceful and serene?
- **Adults.** How do we respond? Do we bring additional anxiety to the situation?

Preventing the behavior

By observing, we may see patterns to their behavior and identify ways we can support our child. Here are some examples:

- **Hungry.** Just before mealtime, give them something hard to snack on before they get too hungry (good for relaxing their nervous system).
- **Teething.** Offer a variety of (cold) teething toys.
- **Needing to explore.** Allow them to explore toys with their mouth.
- **Overstimulating environment.** Reduce the amount of stimulation to make it calmer.
- **Too much noise.** Remove them when we notice that things are becoming too loud.
- **Transitions.** Is the structure of the day predictable enough? Are transitions difficult for them? Allow enough time for them to finish what they are doing. Make sure they get enough free, unstructured play.
- **Protective of their activity.** Model words they can use. They can put their hands on their hips and say, "I'm using this now. It will be available soon."
- **Sensitive to their personal space.** Help them avoid situations where they are cornered or do not have enough personal space.
- **Misguided playfulness.** Some children may bite to be playful or show love, perhaps misunderstanding games such as blowing raspberries on their tummies. Show them other ways to be affectionate, such as cuddles or mutual rough play.
- **Learning social interaction.** If they push another child, they may be wanting to say, "Can we play?" Give them words.
- **Problem with their hearing and eyesight.** A problem with either can feel disorienting for a child, and they may react by being aggressive.
- **Need to relax their nervous system.** Refer to page 155 for ideas on relaxing their nervous system, such as big bear hugs.

Children are very sensitive to our emotions, so we can try to stay confident and not show signs of worry when we are around other children. Our child may sense our anxiety, which will add to their discomfort.

See them every day with fresh eyes and a blank slate. This too will pass.

What to do if they hit/bite/push?

We can be clear that we allow all feelings—toddlers have a lot they need to express—but they cannot hit, bite, or push others. Acknowledge their feelings and remove them from the situation. Once they are calm, we can help them make amends, check that the other child is okay, offer them a tissue if they are crying, or model apologizing.

Here are a couple of examples:

"You look angry. I can't let you bite me. I'm putting you down." We can make sure they are safe while they calm down. Then we can get them to help check that we are okay. "Shall we see if I am hurt? Let's see. Yes, it's a bit red here." If we have allowed enough time for them to become completely calm, they will often want to rub it or give us a kiss.

"You didn't like them touching your hair? I cannot let you hit them. Let's go over here where it is quiet to calm down." Then, once they have had time to calm down, we can help them see if the other child is okay. Or model apologizing. "I'm so sorry that my child hit you. I think he was frustrated, but it's not okay for him to hit you. Are you okay?"

We can help our child explain the problem—for example, that they were playing with the toy the other child took.

Hitting, biting, and pushing phases may require a lot of patience and repetition. We need to remember not to take their behavior personally and be their calm guide during this difficult phase.

What if they laugh after hitting, biting, or pushing?

Children are generally testing a limit by laughing after they hit, bite, or push. They are looking for clear leadership, clarity about what is okay and what is not. We can continue to step in to stop the behavior—calmly and clearly—rather than telling them to stop laughing.

However, if the laughing causes a reaction in us, we can tell them how it makes us feel and find a place to calm down if needed. "It upsets me when you hit me. It's important for me to feel safe. I'm going to make a cup of tea to calm down. I'll be back when I'm feeling better."

And throwing?

Again, this is usually a phase. They want to touch and explore everything around them.

- Look to see if there are any patterns to the behavior.
- Take preventive measures by moving things that they are pushing off tables, placing them on the ground or out of reach. We may need to remove wooden toys that will hurt if thrown for this period.
- Provide opportunities to do lots of throwing at the park or with soft items in the house (socks are excellent for this).
- Be kind, clear, and consistent about what they can throw. "I can't let you throw that inside, but you can throw these little bean bags."

BUILDING CONCENTRATION

> "The essential thing is for the task to arouse such interest that it engages the child's whole personality."
>
> —Dr. Maria Montessori, *The Absorbent Mind*

Concentration is not just a matter of being busy. It means engaging all the senses. To help a toddler build their concentration, we start by observing them to see what they are interested in and learning to master. Then we give them time, possibility, and a prepared environment, and let them repeat the activity and allow them to deepen their concentration.

Tips for building concentration

1. Try to avoid interrupting

Sometimes we comment too much on what the child is doing. We name the puzzle pieces, the colors, and so on. Trust the child. Remain silent when they are working on something. Respond if they look to us.

There are many other moments when we can talk and offer rich language possibilities: when we are out exploring the world together, while preparing and eating meals, and during moments of care, such as bathing. Not when they are in a moment of concentration.

2. Watch what they repeat

Are they opening and closing drawers? Taking objects in and out of baskets? Sorting clothing? Picking up small objects? Collecting rocks? Cleaning the floor? Preparing food? This repetition shows us what they are interested in.

Allow this repetition. Ask them if they would like to repeat it when they have finished. Provide similar opportunities with increasing difficulty.

3. Less is more

Have only a few activities available. Anything that is too easy or too difficult can be put into a storage box and rotated onto the shelves at another time. We will see that children can focus more easily when there is less available. And we can see clearly which activities are no longer being used or which are being thrown—a good sign that we can put them away and bring out another choice.

4. Help as much as is needed and as little as necessary

If we observe that our child is having difficulty, we can wait to see if they can manage themselves. When they are about to give up, we can step in to just give a little bit of help, then step back to see how they get on. This may help them get further with the activity and allow them to continue concentrating. For example, we may be able to help them with turning a key, then step back to see if they can open the box.

5. Have a work area

A floor mat or small table can help a child focus on the activity they have chosen. When they select an activity, there is a small moment when we could help them take it to the mat or table.

However, if they are already working at the shelf, I would not interrupt their concentration. Our interference may be enough to break their concentration completely, and they might walk away from the activity.

DEALING WITH FRUSTRATION

It is common to want to jump in to help our child if they are frustrated. Dr. Montessori used to have some rosary beads she would patiently count to hold herself back from stepping in too quickly.

The child's struggle is important. The child will enjoy mastering activities that are hard enough to provide a challenge, but not so difficult that they'll give up easily. We can wait until they are about to give up and, as before, step in to give a small amount of assistance before stepping back again.

Types of help we can give our child:

- Showing them. "Would you like me to show you?" "Would you like a little help?" Then we could show them slowly (without words) how to, for example, turn a puzzle piece around until it fits.
- Giving a verbal cue. "Have you tried turning it?"

Sometimes they will refuse all help, and their frustration will turn into anger. It's okay for the child to express that, too. They will try again another time.

When we support them in these ways, we recognize that frustration is a part of learning.

WHEN OUR CHILD IS CLINGY

Some children don't want to play by themselves. They won't let us leave the room, even to use the toilet. And the more space we want, the more clingy they get. There can be many reasons why they are clingy:

- The child's temperament. Some children prefer the safety of their parent's company.
- A trip, a change in routine, sickness, a change in work situation, new child care. These big changes can make the child feel cautious.
- Our attention is elsewhere. For example, we're cooking dinner or writing an email.
- They can't manage independently because they lack the skills or access to what they need, or they're reliant on an adult to do things for them.

It is normal for toddlers to need supervision, and they won't be able to play by themselves for hours. It's also important to enjoy time together. But if our child is constantly attached to our leg or wants to be picked up all the time, we can help them play alone for longer periods.

- First, we can play together. Then we can play a little less and watch more. Let them lead the play. Over time, we can sit a little farther away while we watch them.
- Give them our undivided attention and then leave for a moment, telling them that we are going to the kitchen to put the kettle on, going to put laundry in the washer, or something similar. Come straight back. Then pop out again to make the cup of tea or do another little job and come straight back. This gets them used to us going away and coming back.
- When they want to stay with us, don't feel irritated but make it a little bit boring. For example, we can chat with the other parents at a birthday party while they stand with us. If they feel ready, they may go join the other children all by themselves.

Do it together

Include them in daily life. We will find that with age, they will start to play more independently, but in the meantime, we can enjoy that they want to spend time with us.

- Use a stepladder so they can help in the kitchen.
- Let them press the buttons on the washing machine.
- Give them the socks to make into pairs while we do laundry, and so on.
- Our child may say "Mommy do it"—give a little help and step back to see if they can manage the rest themselves. Stay close at first so they still feel safe and secure.

Understand our child

- See things from our child's perspective and acknowledge their feelings. Instead of saying, "Don't worry, it will be okay," we can provide understanding: "Are you feeling scared about this?" This doesn't mean we have to solve the problem; it just lets them know we understand.
- Fill their emotional bucket. Starting the day with a long cuddle and reading books can fill our child's emotional tank before the day gets busy. And when they start to get whiny, rather than looking for more space, we can offer them a cuddle to help them rebalance.
- Our child's "love language" may be touch or spending time together. This child will enjoy a lot of contact with us to feel loved. (See *The Five Love Languages* by Gary Chapman for more on this.)
- An introverted child may find groups overwhelming. They may need to stay with us at first, or we may want to make our visit shorter to accommodate our child's needs.

Make them feel safe

- If we are going somewhere new, give them a little tour when they arrive so they feel oriented.
- Always tell them where we are going rather than sneaking out. "I'm just going to the toilet. I'll be back in two minutes." Our child may cry, but over time they'll begin to trust that we'll come back when we say we will.
- It can help to arrive a little early to parties or group activities. It can be daunting for some children to walk into a room already full of busy children.

I like to think of our child's excursions like petals on a flower, with us at the center. They will make small excursions first, crawling to the other side of the room and coming back; walking farther away as they grow in independence and then coming back; then going off to school and coming back; and one day biking themselves to high school and coming back at the end of the day to check in with us.

If they are clingy, we can help them feel safe enough to explore, maybe just a little before they check in; they will gradually explore longer and go farther, and then they'll be back again soon to check in with us. Even though my children are now teenagers, I am still an important check-in point for them before they head off again to explore further.

SCREEN TIME

In a Montessori approach, we want to offer our toddler many hands-on and firsthand experiences of their world. Screens don't provide such rich sensorial learning.

The website Screen-Free Parenting offers a lot of useful research on screens, including this:

- Young children do not learn language from a screen—they learn language best from a personal relationship with another human.
- Screens can negatively affect children's sleep and attention levels.
- There is concern about physical health—children could spend screen time being active and/or outdoors.

What to do instead

To remove temptation, put screens out of sight and out of reach. We can also be conscious of our own use of screens while our children are around.

If they are bored in a cafe, take them for a walk to see the kitchen staff at work, or bring some books to read and an activity to do together.

Rather than using a screen to help calm our child if they are upset, use the ideas from chapter 6 and they will learn to identify their feelings, learn to calm down, and learn from the difficult times.

My personal experience with screens

My children had very little exposure to screens and electronic toys when they were young. The television was not left on in the background, and we brought along things like books to read when we were out in cafes. From time to time, they saw some carefully selected television programs or short films.

In my children's Montessori school, once the children were 6+ years, there were 2 computers for 30 children, and they would book time if they wanted to research something.

Around the same time, we chose to allow a limited amount of screen time at home. We carefully chose which programs or games they were watching or using, and there was always supervision. This also gave them an idea of what their friends were talking about at school.

For those worried that their child will be left behind, I've found that my children are still very competent on computers. For example, they can build a website, write presentations, and code some simple games with introductory coding programs.

For more ideas about the "whys" and "hows" of limiting screens, I recommend the book *Toxic Childhood: How the Modern World Is Damaging Our Children and What We Can Do About It,* by Sue Palmer. It is very realistic and proactive about how to deal with things like technology with our children.

BILINGUALISM

Because toddlers have an *absorbent mind* and are in a *sensitive period* for language acquisition, it is a wonderful time to expose them to more than one language. They will take in additional languages with little effort, although it does take some effort from the adult to provide language in a consistent way.

If there is more than one language in the home, we can use the *One Person, One Language (OPOL)* approach. Each parent chooses their mother tongue when speaking with the child, while the family uses one agreed-upon "family language."

Here is an example:

A family who lived across the road from me had a child. One parent spoke Italian with the child, the other spoke German with the child, and the parents spoke English with each other. The child also went to a bilingual day care where they were exposed to Dutch and English. The child learned to ask for an apple in Italian with one parent and in German with the other, and if she ever saw me in the street, we would speak in English. (She now goes to a Dutch school where she studies in Dutch, continues to speak Italian and German at home, and speaks less English but has relatively high comprehension.)

We can also use an approach called *Domains of Use*. This is where we have agreed-upon times or places when we use certain languages. For example, on the weekends the family chooses to speak English; out of the home they choose to speak the local language; and at home they speak the parents' mother tongues.

Look at the literacy goals for each of the child's languages. If the goal is to have the child be able to eventually study in a language, they need to spend around 30 percent of the week with that language. Calculate the hours the child is awake and see if it is necessary to increase their exposure in any language. For example, have a teenager read and play with our child in that language, a babysitter who speaks that language, or play groups in that language. Be creative.

Some parents worry that their child will have a language delay if they are being raised to be bilingual. When they have more than one language, the research shows that they should not have any learning delay. For comparison, a 1.5-year-old who is monolingual may have ten words; the bilingual child may have five words in one language and five words in another. So it can appear that their language level is lower, even though they can say ten words in total, too.

The research also does not support parents abandoning their mother tongue to encourage their children to pick up the local language. The mother tongue needs to be strong for any other languages to be acquired. What we can do is increase their exposure to the local language to ensure there is enough input.

I recommend *A Parents' and Teachers' Guide to Bilingualism* by Colin Baker for anyone with questions about bilingualism or learning more than one language.

TO PRACTICE

1. How can we increase connection during daily care?
2. How can we support our child's eating/sleeping/toileting? Can we let go of our anxiety in these areas?
3. Can we keep neutral in conflicts with siblings?
4. How can we build skills with our child
   - around sharing?
   - to interrupt an adult?
   - if they are an introverted child?
   - if they hit/bite/push/throw?
   - to build concentration?
   - to deal with frustration?
   - when they are clingy?

When we apply Montessori principles at home in this way, we are learning to be the child's guide. We are kind and clear when needed. We help them scaffold the skills they will need. And we cultivate connection with our child every day.

BEING THE ADULT

8

PREPARATION OF THE ADULT

Dr. Montessori was well aware of the work we need to do on ourselves. She called this *preparation of the adult*. How can we be the best model for our children? How can we stay calm with an unpredictable toddler in the home? What might we be bringing to the situation? What unresolved issues are showing up here?

We are not aiming to be perfect parents. When I tried to be (or appeared to be) a perfect parent, I was stressed and disconnected from my family, busy worrying about everything. Rather, we are aiming to have fun and feel relaxed with our families, starting from where we are today. Maybe some of these ideas can help us to parent from a calmer place—a place where we can support and guide our toddler.

We cannot change our partner, only how we react to them. The same is true with our children. Who knew that parenting would become an almost spiritual journey?

And what a journey it is. Sometimes I wish I had known all of this before I became a parent. Yet, we know only what we know. So I think of how I've grown up alongside my children—that they see me trying and getting it wrong and trying again and getting a bit better, constantly learning and growing.

What I have learned may not work for every family. I don't want to tell other people how to live. Instead, I'd like to share some of my practices that have helped me as a parent and Montessori teacher, including apologizing and "doing it over" when I get it wrong.

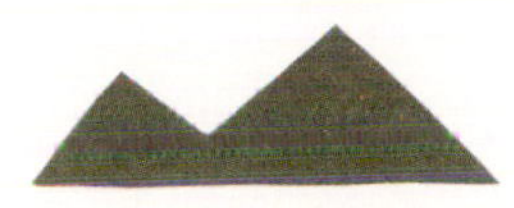

PHYSICAL SELF-CARE

We do best when we keep our bodies, our minds, and our souls strong and healthy. To nurture our families, we must also nurture ourselves.

We need good food. Some movement (perhaps biking around town or chasing our toddler in the park). Time outside every day. Maybe long baths in the evening when no one can disturb us. We can always look for new ways to add fun or peace to our day.

We can acknowledge the guilt we may feel about putting ourselves first. And let it go. Reframe it instead as being a great example for our children to look after themselves.

If we are feeling tired or burned out, we can get help. Pushing past our limit is not a sustainable long-term option. The help could be a babysitter, a grandparent, a friend who will swap with us, a partner. Our toddler will learn that there are other special people in their life whom we trust and with whom they will be safe. So it's a win-win.

If we are feeling depressed, we should absolutely get help from a doctor, even if it is just to see what options are available. I remember turning up at the doctor when both my children were still under 2, worried I might be depressed. It helped to have someone to talk to and to care for me when I was so busy looking after others. If the depression is concerning, a doctor will help to figure out the next steps.

CULTIVATE A LEARNING MIND-SET

We don't undertake any paid job without some training, and we expect that our child's schoolteachers will continue their professional development. So, as a parent, we can keep learning, too. (By reading this book, you are already cultivating a learning mind-set about raising your child.)

In addition, we can:

- Learn more about our child's unique development.
- Research things that are different about our child and get the support we need.
- Find a training like a positive discipline training or a course in nonviolent communication.
- Explore many and varied books and resources. (See my recommendations on pages 218 and 219.) Perhaps try listening to podcasts and audiobooks.
- Read and learn things that have nothing to do with raising children. We need to have our own rich life as well.
- Learn to follow our intuition. Our thinking brain is so strong these days, so switching it off and listening to our intuition—that calm voice inside—is another skill we can practice.

START AND END THE DAY RIGHT

My morning and evening rituals probably have the biggest effect on how I show up as a parent. It's not strict, but it's fairly consistent most days. It helps me be intentional about how I live each day, rather than reacting to what life throws at me. If I can get in good "alignment" at the beginning of the day, it sets me up for the rest of the day.

Even when my children were toddlers, I would try to wake up half an hour before anyone else in the house so I could have some quiet time for myself.

If we can't be awake before the rest of the family, consider how we can create a morning routine that we love that includes them. This might be morning snuggles, reading books, having breakfast together, putting on some happy music, or making a cup of coffee or tea to drink while we are all getting ready for our day.

When I wake up before the rest of the family, I use the time in the following ways:

- I lie in my bed to meditate—it's impossible to be bad at it. Some days I notice my mind is super active, and other days I manage to focus on my breath for longer. This practice really helps me be less reactive during the day. And on those scattered days, I can come back to that drop of peace I was able to find in the morning.
- I spend five minutes writing:
  - things I am grateful for and appreciate.
  - a few things that would make the day amazing (things I actually have control over and that can be as simple as having a cup of coffee or sitting outside on the steps).
  - my intention for the day (for example, to choose ease, to listen to others, or to focus on love and connection).
- With any time that is remaining, I start to get dressed before I hear the sound of lovely children's feet.

If I am interrupted before I am finished, I try to think of it as a reminder of how lucky I am to have a lovely family and to hear the sounds of them coming to join me.

At the end of the day, I take a bath and read a book. I write down three amazing things that happened and an intention for the next day.

We may not think we have time, but it is possible if we make it a priority. I do this before I read the news or check social media. It makes a big difference in how I can be my best self.

We can set aside some time to think through what morning and night rituals serve us best. Just as we look after our families, we will benefit from looking after our own well-being in the same way.

PRACTICE PRESENCE

It's difficult to stay present when we are trying to be all things to all people and being pulled in lots of directions as adults with lots of commitments, including as parents.

Here are some ways to practice being present:

- **Focus on doing one task at a time.** I know I'm not really listening to my children about their day if I have my back to them while I am preparing something in the kitchen. It works better for all of us if I tell them that I'd love to hear what they have to say as soon as I am finished. Or stop what I am doing, listen, and then finish what I am doing.
- **Use a notebook.** I always have a few notebooks to write down things I think of when I am playing a board game with the children or running one of my classes. It's written down for when I can look at it at a later time. I "process" the notes later, leaving my mind free to be present.
- **Use technology consciously.** I love technology. Yet we rarely switch off from it. So I often hide my phone in my bedroom so that I don't pick it up to check it as I pass by or as soon as it beeps. Anytime I pick up my phone for one task, I inevitably start looking at some other app.
- **Calm the mind.** It's not only technology. It's also our mind. It's really hard to stay in the here and now. We continually play back moments from the past and make plans for the future. We can make ourselves crazy.

Right now, here, in the present moment, there is nothing to worry about. Hold this book and just breathe in. Then breathe out. For that short moment there was nothing to think about. Being present. Still. I love it when my mind quiets like that.

Imagine if we could spend more time in that peaceful space. With practice we can.

The more we can practice making space for these moments, the easier it is for us to slow down, to observe our child, to see things from their perspective. The more time we spend finding a calm space inside ourselves, the easier it will be for us to return to that space when we need to be a calm leader for our child while they are having a hard time.

And guess who is great at being in the present moment to help us practice? Our toddlers.

Remember how they squeal with excitement at the sound of an airplane. How they find flowers to pick in the most unexpected of places. How they wriggle their toes in the grass at the park.

Follow them and learn.

OBSERVATION

As discussed in chapter 5, observation is a tool Montessori teachers use a lot. We discussed how we can make factual observations at home, too, to allow us to let go of judgment, bias, and other analysis.

I include it again here because observation can help us:

- remove our judgment of the situation, which stops us from being triggered by our child's behavior, and allows us to respond rather than react. (Instead of "They are always dropping their bowl on the floor," we observe, "The bowl dropped onto the floor.")
- really see our child objectively with fresh eyes
- be more present and notice more details about our child and the world around us
- connect with our child as we see things from their perspective and gain a greater understanding of them

If we are feeling wound up, we can grab a notebook and observe. If we have our hands full, we can try to observe without writing it down. Stay away from analysis, and enjoy the present moment observing our child.

FILL OUR EMOTIONAL BUCKET AND OUR CHILD'S

We all have an emotional bucket. Our emotional bucket is full when we feel safe, secure, loved, and accepted. It needs to be continuously refilled. When we neglect our emotional buckets, we become more reactive.

We are responsible for filling our own buckets, for finding ways to look after ourselves, and for making sure we are receiving the help and support we need. Our partners are not the only ones who can help here. With a little creativity, we can come up with lots of ways to fill our bucket.

Some ideas:

- make a cup of tea or coffee
- play some music
- have a Skype conversation with grandparents
- go outside
- invite friends around for a meal
- bake something
- arrange a night out (by ourselves, with our partner, with friends)
- do a babysitting swap with a friend

When our bucket is full, it is easier to fill our child's bucket. The easiest way to fill a child's bucket is with connection—making them feel the belonging, significance, and acceptance we discussed in chapter 5. We can spend some time reading books with them, have a snuggle in our pajamas, laugh. This fills our child's emotional bucket (and our own) and helps them be more receptive and less reactive throughout the day.

SLOW DOWN

Going slowly is a tool we can use in our daily life to live with more ease with a toddler, older children, and our family.

We speed through our days, often worried we'll miss out on something. Yet, I know how much more I get out of every day when I slow down and use all my senses: smell the rain in the air before a storm, feel the wind on my cheeks as I cycle through the city, taste and enjoy every bite of food rather than eating on the run, and so on.

We will have to figure out what is really important to us and what will have to wait or not happen at all.

For me, going slowly means things like:

- sitting down for a cup of tea when I get home from class rather than immediately starting on the innumerable tasks waiting for me
- putting on some music to make the moment richer
- cooking wholesome food and enjoying the cooking process, remembering to savor the tastes as I eat
- not putting too many things in my calendar so I don't have to rush from one thing to the next

- saying "no" to a lot, so I can say "yes" to more time with my family and friends and, sometimes, the couch
- being selective about what I work on, choosing only things I enjoy and that will have the most impact
- reading every night
- a weekend of travel to new places and in nature to recharge, and taking in more of an impression than having to see everything—the simpler the better

Toddlers will appreciate our slower pace, making it easier for them to absorb all that is around them.

Here are some examples:

- When dressing, first allow them to try; then step in to show them when they need help, using slow, precise movements.
- Slow down when we show our child how to carry a basket or a tray—use two hands so they can be successful themselves when they try.
- Slowly move chairs using two hands.
- When singing together, sing slowly and do the actions slowly as well. This allows time for our child to process and perhaps join us in singing or doing the actions.
- If we ask our child to do something, like sitting down to eat, count to ten in our head before repeating to allow time for the child to process our request.
- Go slowly when we are encouraging our child's curiosity, too (see chapter 5)—going at their pace, rushing less, and saving more time for play and exploration.

For more ideas, I enjoyed the book *In Praise of Slow* by Carl Honoré. It's not at all scientific, just one person's attempt to try out different genres from the slow movement philosophy. Spoiler alert! The final chapter is my favorite. It concludes that it is ideal to go slowly most of the time so when we do need to hurry, our children will be more accommodating.

One last thing. Unless our child is in immediate danger, there is generally enough time to at least count to three in our head before reacting to any situation. Pretend to be Dr. Montessori counting rosary beads before rushing in to help. Go slowly.

It will allow us to **respond rather than react**.

BE MY GUIDE
I DON'T NEED
A SERVANT
OR A BOSS

BE THE CHILD'S GUIDE

When my son was 1 year old, I read the book *How to Talk So Kids Will Listen and Listen So Kids Will Talk*. (I've referred to it throughout this book, if that is any indication of what an effect it had, and continues to have, on me.)

The biggest takeaway for me was realizing that my role as a parent is not to rush in to solve every problem for my children. Rather, we can be there to support them, be their sounding board, or be their safe place to release whatever frustrations they have had in their day.

This is an enormous shift. And a huge weight off my shoulders. We are the children's guide, planting the seeds but letting them grow. We are their rock in the background, helping only as much as is necessary but as little as possible.

A guide:

- gives space for the child to work it out for themselves
- is available when needed
- is respectful, kind, and clear
- will help a child take responsibility when needed
- will provide a safe, rich environment to explore
- listens
- responds rather than reacts

We don't need to be a boss giving them orders, directing them, or teaching them everything they need to learn. And we don't need to be their servant doing everything for them.

We can simply be their guide.

USE OUR HOME AS A HELPER

Just as a Montessori teacher uses the classroom environment as the second teacher (see chapter 2), we can set up our homes to help us as well. We've discussed how to do this in detail in chapter 4, but I'd like to return to some of those ideas here to illustrate how the changes we make to support our child can support us as well.

When we are feeling tired, we can look for ways that our home can do more of the work for us. Here are a few examples:

- If we find that our child is overly reliant on us, then we can look for ways to add independence into our daily rhythm.
- Every time we do something for our toddler that they can do themselves, we can make a small change so they can do it successfully by themselves—eventually taking away some of the burden on us. For example, we can add a scoop to a container so they can serve their own cereal at breakfast time. If they pull all the tissues onto the floor, we can look for a way to put out a few at a time on a dish and keep the box out of reach. The options are limited only by our imagination.
- If we find that we are saying "no" a lot, we can look for ways to change the environment.
- If we find that we are spending a lot of time tidying up, we can look for ways to reduce the number of toys available. We can make more thoughtful selections, observe what our child is no longer interested in, or find ways to support scaffolding the skills necessary for our child to clean up after themselves.

BE HONEST

Our children learn more from watching us than from us telling them how to behave. So we want to model honesty with our children. We want them to learn that being truthful is an important value in our home. No white lies.

I'd say most people think they are honest. Yet, little white lies are common:

- "Tell them I'm on the phone." (When we don't want to speak to someone.)
- "What do I think of your haircut? It looks great." (When we don't think that at all.)
- "I don't have any money on me." (To a person asking for money on the street.)

Instead we could say:

- To an unwanted call, "I'm tired right now. Can I call you back tomorrow?/Can you send me an email?"
- About someone's new haircut, "You look really happy with it."
- To a person on the street, "Not today—good luck" or "Can I buy you some fruit in the shop?"

It is actually really hard to be kind and truthful. It's something to strive to model.

TAKE RESPONSIBILITY FOR OUR LIFE AND CHOICES

There are many things that are difficult or challenging about life that we cannot change. But we can acknowledge it when some of life's headaches are a result of choices we've made.

If we choose to live in a house with a garden, it will require maintenance. Or if we choose to live in a cosmopolitan city, it means rents are high. Or if we want a nontraditional education for our children, it may cost money. We don't have to change these choices. Indeed, we are lucky to be able to make choices about these things at all. We can own these choices and the resulting responsibilities.

We can also model accepting responsibility for our choices to our children, commenting out loud when we run into a frustrating problem. "The train is late again! I'm grateful to live in a city with public transportation, but I'm not feeling very patient today. Next time we could leave earlier." We can observe ourselves neutrally and, with some distance, calm down and adjust our perspective.

We can take all the shoulds out of our life and do only the things we want to do. "I should iron these shirts." "I should cook the children's dinner." "I should call her back." "I should pay more attention to my children." This may seem like I'm advising against cooking dinner or paying attention to our children. Rather, I'm saying we cook dinner because we want to provide a nutritious home-cooked dinner for our children. Own that choice. I'm saying we pay attention to our children because we want them to grow up feeling secure and accepted. Own that, too.

Every time we say "should," we can think about whether it's important to us. Otherwise we can be creative and change it. And for the things we cannot change, we can see these as opportunities to be creative. If we work full-time, we can apply these ideas on the weekends, during mealtimes and bath times, and on our morning drop-off. If we cannot afford a school that offers the perfect setting, we can find one that complements our family values. And if we can't find that, we can keep applying the principles from this book to our daily life.

We can figure out what is important and preserve it. When we take ownership of our life and our choices, we are steering the ship that is our life rather than pulling the ropes senselessly against the storm.

LEARN FROM OUR MISTAKES

When we make a mistake, it is easy to blame someone or something else. For example, our toddler drove us crazy so we lost our temper, or the map was not clear so we went the wrong way. Just as we take ownership of our choices, we need to own our mistakes as well. There are days we are not going to have as much patience. When we get things wrong. When we do something that means we let our child down, our partner down, ourselves down.

Making mistakes means that we have an opportunity to apologize. And to think about what we could have done instead. I can always say to my child (or anyone, for that matter), "I'm so sorry. I should not have . . . What I could have said/done is . . ." This sets a far stronger example for our child than blaming someone else. They see that we can learn from our mistakes, and it shows that we are always trying to make kinder choices. And that no one, not even their parent, is perfect.

CELEBRATE WHERE WE ARE

We can be so busy trying to improve things that we forget to reflect on the present. I know that I forget to acknowledge and accept where I am right now while I am striving to learn more and be a better model for my child.

We often forget to say to ourselves, *We are enough. We are doing our best.*

I like to imagine that we are all full glasses of water. Rather than looking to others to fill our glass—our partner, our children, our work—we are full just as we are.

That gives me a huge sense of relief. It doesn't mean that I will stop learning and stop improving, but I feel okay with who I am today. That means I feel like I can be more to those in my life, including my children.

I also like to think of our toddlers as full glasses. They are doing the best they can in their little bodies where they are today. We can support them without being frustrated by them or angry with them.

SELF-AWARENESS

To parent in this way takes an increasing amount of self-awareness. In our Montessori training, this is part of self-observation.

We need to **recognize when our limits are about to be tested** and find a way to assert our limits—with kindness and clarity. If we let a situation build up, and we get irritated, it is almost impossible to calmly step in and provide clear guidance.

It's okay to have limits. It is part of being aware of ourselves and our needs, and balancing them with the needs of our children and others in our family. (See chapter 9 on working together with others.)

When we **find ourselves being triggered**, we can observe ourselves. Are we taking on our child's problem? Is it bringing up something that we don't like about ourselves?

We can step back to take a look objectively or write it down so we can figure it out later, when we are calm. We can give ourselves compassion and see which of our needs are not being met (for example, need for connection or to be cared for), and brainstorm ways to meet those needs.

Then we can move back to being the guide, the confident leader, the rock our child needs us to be.

KEEP PRACTICING

All the ideas in this book will take practice. Being this way with our child is like learning a new language and takes a whole lot of practice. I'm still practicing, and my children are becoming young adults, and I've been working as a Montessori teacher for years.

But it does get easier and more natural every day.

> "The child developing harmoniously and the adult improving himself at his side make a very exciting and attractive picture . . . This is the treasure we need today—helping the child become independent of us and make his way by himself and receiving in return his gifts of hope and light."
>
> —Dr. Maria Montessori, *Education and Peace*

TO PRACTICE

1. What brings us into alignment during the day? Are we happy? Are our needs being met?
2. Can we be more present? Slower?
3. Can we shift from being our child's boss or servant to being their guide?
4. Can we use our home to save us some work?
5. Are we blaming others for our life situation? Can we take responsibility for our choices? Or change them?
6. Can we celebrate where we are today?

9

WORKING TOGETHER

WHAT ABOUT EVERYONE ELSE?

We don't parent alone. There are many ways of being in a family—married, partners, single parent, living with grandparents, opposite or same-sex parents, divorced, from different cultural backgrounds, and so on. The number and types of family constellations will only grow as our society evolves.

No matter what our family constellation, we live in the context of the people around us as well—an extended family. These may or may not be blood relatives but could also include friends, friends from parenting groups, school friends, or the people in the local shop where we purchase our groceries. These are the people in the life of our family.

Many questions come up when we are parenting alone, with a partner, and with extended family.

- Maybe we have read this book and would love our "family" to also try some of the ideas mentioned here. How do we get them on board?
- What are our family values, anyway?
- Do we listen and speak to our family as we do to our toddler?
- Where do an adult's feelings stand in this child-driven approach?
- What if our toddler prefers one parent?
- What about a grandparent or caregiver? How can they apply this approach?
- What if we are separated from our partner? How will it affect our child? And how can it remain a positive experience for the child?

These are important questions. Here are some thoughts that align with the Montessori approach to get us started.

PARENTS ARE PEOPLE, TOO

It is easy to end up making life all about the children. We put our own needs on hold or feel guilty if we do something for ourselves.

We are all people, deserving of having our needs met. Following the child does not mean ignoring ourselves. Work together with our child. Be assertive if we need to be.

We allow our children a lot of freedom. But we can express our needs, too—for example, wanting some peace in the evening while our child rests in bed. (You may wish to refer to the table of feelings and needs on page 232.)

Make time for the adult relationship. Our partner, if we have one, is a person, too. And that relationship is very important. Without it, we might not have become a parent in the first place. However, we often forget to prioritize it.

I love the example I once heard about a French family with four children. When the parent who was working outside the home returned to the house each evening, the parents would sit down and have a glass of wine, check in, and connect with each other for about ten minutes rather than rushing to prepare dinner and into the usual evening routine. The parents did not jump up to rush to their children's rescue during this time. Their children learned that this was their parents' special time. They were showing their children that their relationship was important.

And that their parents are people, too.

PREFERRING ONE PARENT

Toddlers and children may go through phases of favoring one parent. They want only this parent to bathe them, read to them, dress them, or tuck them into bed.

If this continues, it can be upsetting and alienating for the other parent.

There is no one-size-fits-all approach to this situation, but here are some things to consider.

Is the child looking for a reaction? I think in many of these cases, the toddler is looking for clarity and is testing limits. We don't need to react or give in to their demands. If they push away one parent, that parent can gently acknowledge the toddler's feelings. "You wanted someone else to help you. And I'm helping you today." Remain calm, gentle, and confident.

Look for changes at home. If one parent has been traveling a lot, or there is a change at home like a new baby or moving to a different house, this can be the way the child expresses themselves; it's one thing they can try to control when everything else is out of their control. It does not mean that we need to change caregivers to meet their demands. But they may need some extra understanding and cuddles, and for us to see things from their perspective.

THE KEY TO WORKING TOGETHER AS A FAMILY

I believe the key to working together as a family is to recognize that each one of us has needs and to be creative in finding ways to make sure everyone's needs are met. It won't be easy, but it's possible. Or at least we can start the conversation.

Working with our child

The adult is in charge, but the child can definitely have input into how to solve problems. "You really want to keep playing outside, and I'm ready to go in. **How can we solve the problem?**" We can do this even with preverbal children. Revisit chapter 6 for specific suggestions.

Working with our partner

I truly think that, with some flexibility and understanding, everyone's needs can be met.

Let's take a regular weekend afternoon as an example. It is time to go to the supermarket, the children would like to go to the playground, our partner would like a nap, and we would like to meet a friend for a coffee.

Rather than bribing the children by saying, "We'll go to the park if you are good," we can choose to plan something for everyone that is **not conditional**. Perhaps we can go to the supermarket without the children and then take them to the playground while our partner naps. Or we order the groceries online and our friend comes to visit us at home while the children play and our partner naps. Any combination or other solution is possible.

Working with others

Our toddlers will have other people to care for them other than us. They may have a grandparent or babysitter look after them, or they may go to day care or school.

They will learn that there are other people in the world whom their parents trust with their care. They will learn to trust others. And they will learn a lot from other people's knowledge of the world. The child's world will be enriched by these interactions.

When we find someone we trust with the care of our toddler, our child will sense it. The best advice I received from my children's Montessori preschool teacher was to give them a big positive, yet short, goodbye. "Have a lot of fun and I'll see you after story time." I think I said the same thing every day. It reassured me, and it reassured them. When they ran out of class, I'd welcome them with a hug if they wanted it and say, "It's so lovely to see you." I did not need to tell them how much I missed them—that is a lot for a toddler to carry.

What they do need is the message that their parent trusts this person, so they trust them, too.

They also need to trust us in this process, so we should let them know if we are leaving and be okay with the fact that this may cause them some sadness. This is easier for the child than disappearing without telling them, having them suddenly notice we aren't there, and not being able to understand where we have gone or when we are coming back.

GETTING FAMILY ON BOARD

It is impossible to change someone else: not our children, our partner, or our family. We want them to take on these Montessori ideas. Yet we cannot force this upon them.

Do not despair.

We can start with ourselves. I often think the best thing we can do is to keep practicing. Often people will notice that we are parenting differently, and then ask for more information. "I see that you did not shout at your child when he was upset in the playground. Can you tell me more?" We are models not only for our children, but for others around us. Some will be curious and ask. But not everyone. That's okay, too.

Find different ways to share the information. Pass along a short article. Share a story about someone who is following a similar approach. Find a radio program or podcast episode that touches on one aspect that might resonate. Pass on this book. Forward a newsletter. Watch an online workshop with them. Get them to come to an in-person workshop at a Montessori school. Have conversations. Drip. Drip. Drip. Slow and steady information, easy to digest, in small doses, at a pace they are open to trying.

Watch how we talk with our family. Often we want our family to speak to our child in a gentle way, without correcting them, limiting criticism, and encouraging them. Then we end up talking to, and listening to, our family in exactly the way we are trying not to with our child. We correct them if they say the wrong thing. We get frustrated at their impatience. We end up talking over them and not showing them respect.

Acknowledge our family's feelings and translate for them. No one is right and no one is wrong. Just as we have learned to see from our child's perspective, we can also learn to see from the perspective of members of our family.

We may not like the way they talk or interact with our child, but we can always translate for them.

"It sounds like Grandad does not want you to climb on the couch."
"It sounds like your mother does not want you to throw your food."
"You two are having a hard time with each other. Let me know if you want me to help."

We can use the same idea on the playground, with neighbors, or with relatives with whom we may not agree. We can translate for them, too.

Go for agreement on the big family values. With enough wisdom, we can have conversations in which our family can find points of agreement. For example, we may find that we all want the best for the child. That we want them to grow up to be respectful and responsible. That we want them to be curious but that we all have our own limits.

Within this big picture, our toddler will learn that **each person in their family has their own unique approach**. Indeed, they will learn naturally who to go to when they want to be silly, who to go to when not everything is right in their world, and so on.

What a lucky child to have so many people caring for them. Even if we are not in contact with our immediate family, they can receive a lot of care from the village around us.

GRANDPARENTS AND CAREGIVERS

If you are a grandparent or caregiver, this section is for you. You can apply any of the techniques mentioned in this book.

At first this approach may seem very different from the one you are used to and that may have served you well with your own children. Here are a few easy ways to start. If you like this approach, you can learn more about it by reading more of this book.

1. **Watch the child.** Take your cues from them. What are they interested in? Is it okay for them to explore freely? How can you let them explore while making sure they are safe?

2. **See if they can work it out themselves.** Whether it is trying to feed or dress themselves or struggling with a toy, give them a little time to see if they can figure it out themselves. The joy on their face when they manage is priceless.

3. **What do you enjoy that you may be able to share with them?** Sharing your interests can help the child have rich experiences. Do you play an instrument? Have some beautiful handcraft materials they can explore? Enjoy playing a sport that you could simplify to show them?

4. **Explore outside.** If you are worried about them breaking something or keeping them entertained, head outside to a park, playground, or walking trail, or simply walk to the local shops. Let them show you everything they see—you can name what they show you—and talk about it.

5. **Give feedback about what you see.** Rather than simply praising them by saying, "Good job," let them know what you saw. "I saw you swinging all by yourself." "You ran all the way to the top of the hill and rolled down. That looked like fun." We are trying to allow them to judge for themselves rather than to look for external approval.

6. **Give your presence, not your presents.** Gift giving can be fun. It can show your love. But what shows your love even more than another toy is your time. If you really want to buy a gift, consider buying tickets for the zoo so you can visit together, a book you can enjoy on the couch, or a gift card for their parents to have a meal while you babysit. Having less stuff means we can stay on this planet longer together. We want to show our children how to care for their environment, as well as for themselves and others.

7. **What values do you share with their parents?** This common ground is a good place to start. It will show some consistency for the toddler who likes order. Some of your rules may be different, which the toddler will learn. As long as the big picture is the same, the child will feel safe and secure in their relationship with both you and their parents.

8. **Can you give the parents a sense of belonging, significance, and acceptance?** Usually differences of opinion within the extended family (caregivers included) indicate a longing for acceptance. Even adults have an inner child wanting to be loved and accepted for who we are. Showing the child's parents that you understand their perspective can go a long way toward creating space for the differences.

WHEN THERE IS CONFLICT IN THE FAMILY

To help us communicate our concerns and hear the concerns of the other member(s) of the family, try this active listening exercise. All that is needed is to ask the other party if they have twenty minutes. This technique is adapted from Dr. Scilla Elworthy's keynote address at the 2017 Montessori Congress.

For the first five minutes, the other person can talk about whatever is bothering them. Listen, hear what they say, and notice the feelings that are coming up for them.

For the following five minutes, we tell them what we heard them say and what we think they were feeling. They can let us know if we misunderstood anything.

Then we switch roles. Now we can talk for five minutes about anything that is bothering us, while they listen.

In the last five minutes, they let us know what we said and any feelings they noticed coming up for us. We can also let them know if they didn't understand anything correctly.

If it feels like the conflict would benefit from another session, we may want to repeat the process for another twenty minutes.

We will start to see the other person and their needs and how we are all human and just want to get our needs met.

Tip 1

Try to avoid language that blames the other person. For example, say, "It's important for me to be respected" rather than "You don't respect me." Use "I" statements, make observations, and identify feelings and needs.

Tip 2

Make requests, not demands, of others. There are always many ways to solve a problem if we are creative, so be open to other solutions, too.

You can find a table of feelings and needs in the appendix (see page 232).

DIVORCE DOES NOT HAVE TO BE A DIRTY WORD

When parents decide to separate, it is possible to transition to an amicable family arrangement where the child simply has two parents living in different homes. Ideally, a co-parenting arrangement can be reached where parents have shared responsibility and both have time with the child.

Even in the 1900s, Dr. Montessori acknowledged that both parents played an important role for the child, as long as there is no psychological or physical reason for a child not to have contact with one of the parents. The child's safety is the first priority.

There is still a stigma around separation and divorce. It is sad when a relationship between parents ends. But it does not have to be negative. In fact, if both parents are happier as a result, it can be a more positive experience for the child who, even at a young age, can sense the atmosphere in the house when there is fighting, disagreement, and disharmony.

Stability is important for the child at this time. Have a regular schedule with each parent so the child knows what to expect. We have discussed how toddlers have a strong sense of order. Make it a priority.

Be honest with the child in an age-appropriate way. Don't assume they are too young to know what is going on. On the other hand, they don't need to know all the details. Be factual and keep them involved and updated as the situation evolves.

Being kind about the other parent in the child's company is critical. The parents' commitment to speaking kindly to and about each other when the child is present is paramount. Sometimes it will be very difficult, in which case we can physically step away from the conflict and discuss the matter later. We can talk to our friends, our family, or a counselor about difficulties we are having with the other parent, but not to the child. It is not fair to put the child in the middle.

Remember, we are both still the child's parents, their family; we're just not living together.

TO PRACTICE

1. Are our needs being met? If not, brainstorm ways to meet our needs.
2. Is there a way that everyone in the family can have their needs met? Be creative.
3. What ideas would help to get family on board?
4. Are there any conflicts that need to be resolved? Try the exercise from the section "When there is conflict in the family" (see page 200).

WHAT'S NEXT

10

GETTING READY FOR PRESCHOOL/SCHOOL

Here are a few tips for those families who will be getting ready for preschool or school soon, particularly if the child will be going to a Montessori school.

The first thing is to **practice skills of independence**. For example, we can look for ways to support putting on their own jacket, being able to get their shoes on and off by themselves, and learning to wipe their nose.

Next is to **practice separation**. Particularly if there has not been another caregiver helping with the toddler, we will want to practice this skill just as we would any other skill. We can start with having someone come to our house to read and play together. Once the child is comfortable with them, we could make a short trip to run errands (being sure to tell them as we are leaving, even if our child is sad about it). They will learn that we come back. We can build up to longer periods apart until they are used to being away from us for the same amount of time as they will be at school.

Finally, something they will do throughout their lives is **practicing social skills**. At the playground, we can help translate for them so they learn to use their words, guide them to stand up for themselves if needed, and model care of others. This will provide them with the support they need to be ready to learn how to get along with, and care for, others in their new school.

Montessori materials at home

When our child starts school, it's best not to have the same Montessori materials at home. There are several reasons for this:

- They may be spending up to six hours a day at school and will be much more engaged with using and learning from the materials if they are found only in their classroom.
- We do not want to present the materials in a way that is different from how they learn at school—this may be confusing for them.
- They also need time for unstructured playtime, time outside, being involved in our daily lives, and simply catching up with friends.

The one Montessori activity from the classroom that my children's Montessori teacher said was okay to do at home was to play "I spy with my little eye something beginning with . . ." The only difference from regular "I spy" is that this game uses the phonetic sound of the letter rather than its name. For example, *buh* is used instead of *b* for a ball, *tr* instead of *t* for a tree.

THE COMING YEARS

Dr. Montessori developed an overview of a child's development from the age of 0 to 24 years based on her scientific observations. She called this the *four planes of development*.

It may be a surprise that she considered us children until the age of 24. Now brain research shows that the prefrontal cortex of the brain—the area for rational decision making and controlling social behavior—keeps developing until our early twenties. More than a hundred years later, brain research is backing up what Dr. Montessori observed.

In each plane of development, with each plane being six years in length, Dr. Montessori recognized similarities in a child's physical, psychological, and behavioral development.

Let's see what lies ahead after the toddler years.

Infancy (0 to 6 years): the first plane of development

The purpose of these first six years is for the child to gain physical and biological independence from their parent. With such enormous changes taking place during this time, it is generally a very volatile period.

The child goes through significant physical change in this period—growing from a baby entirely dependent on an adult into a child able to walk, talk, and eat by themselves.

Moving toward independence also means sometimes wanting to be close to the parent and other times pushing us away or wanting to do everything for themselves—a kind of crisis of independence. The child also does a lot of testing to make sense of the world around them.

The absorbent mind is also active during this whole period, with children from birth to 6 years being able to absorb all the information around them like a sponge. In the first three years of this cycle (0–3 years) the child absorbs this information completely unconsciously and without effort—i.e., with an *unconscious absorbent mind*. In the second three years (3–6 years) the child becomes a conscious learner, the *conscious absorbent mind*.

What does this mean in practice? The child moves from simply accepting and adapting to the world around him (0–3 years) to a child asking *why* and *how* (3–6 years). They want to understand all that they have taken in during the first three years. They also become fascinated by other cultures and enjoy maps of the world, flags, and landforms. They may also show interest in reading, writing, and mathematics using concrete learning materials.

They are sensorial learners in this plane, even in the womb. From 0 to 3 they are using all their senses to explore the world around them. From 3 to 6 they begin to classify these sensations, for example, big and small, hard and soft, rough and smooth, or loud and quiet.

They are based in reality in this period—they understand most easily the world they see around them and are fascinated with seeing how things work. Imaginative play may be seen from around 2.5+ years as they make sense of the world around them, for example, playing store or families.

This period is also when the child lays down their personality. Their experience in these early years will greatly shape who they are in their adult years.

We are indeed planting the seeds . . .

Childhood (6 to 12 years): the second plane of development

Where the first-plane child was working on physical and biological independence, the second-plane child is working on their mental independence. They are driven to know everything and to explore the reason behind things, no longer simply absorbing the information.

They are beginning to develop independent thought about the world around them and developing their moral sense. They start to explore the gray areas. "Is it right or wrong?" "Is it fair or unfair?"

They explore the world with their imagination—able to understand history and to project ideas into the future. This is also a collaborative age where they love to work in groups around large tables or on the floor.

There is not so much rapid growth in this period, so it might be nice for parents to hear that this is a more stable period and the child is less volatile. The foundation is already laid in the first six years when we set clear limits; in the second plane, our child understands the limits and does not need to challenge them every time.

The stem is growing tall and strong . . .

Adolescence (12 to 18 years): the third plane of development

The adolescent period has much in common with the first plane, so for parents who think that toddlers and teenagers are similar, Dr. Montessori would agree.

Again this is a period of enormous physical and psychological change as children move through puberty. And where the infant was becoming physically independent from their parent, the teenager is working on social independence and moving away from their families. There is a struggle between sometimes wanting to be part of the family and other times wanting to be independent—another crisis of independence, this time of a social variety.

Teenagers love sharing ideas and their ideals with others, particularly ways in which they would change the world (including developing social policy). Interestingly, Dr. Montessori observed that they are not actually as academic in this period, at a time when traditional schools generally become more academic.

Instead, Dr. Montessori proposed an *Erdkinder*, or farm school, as the perfect learning environment for a teenager. There they could learn by working the land, selling their goods at market, and figuring out their place in a social group. There are Montessori high schools in cities, known as "urban compromises." They try to apply similar principles in a city setting.

I want to add a personal note here to say that puberty and teenagers do not have to be scary. I found that having two teenagers in the house was a pleasure, and they were lovely people to spend time with.

Leaves and blossoms unfurl, nearing maturity . . .

Maturity (18 to 24 years): the fourth plane of development

Dr. Montessori said that if everything has been done in the first three planes of development, the fourth plane takes care of itself. She referred to this plane's work as developing spiritual and moral independence.

These young adults primarily want to give back to society, for example, through volunteer work or the Peace Corps. They may enter college and join the workforce.

Similar to the second plane of development, this is a more stable period, and the young adult has a reasoning, logical mind. They are busy exploring areas of interest in work and study at a deep level.

And their brains are nearly completely formed.

The plant is fully grown, still requiring our care and attention, but now completely independent of us.

FOUR PLANES OF DEVELOPMENT

FIRST PLANE	SECOND PLANE	THIRD PLANE	FOURTH PLANE
0–6 years	6–12 years	12–18 years	18–24 years
We are planting the seeds.	The stem is growing tall and strong.	Leaves and blossoms unfurl, nearing maturity.	The plant is fully grown.
• physical and biological independence • absorbent mind • concrete understanding of the world • sensorial learner • children work in parallel with small amounts of collaboration • rapid growth and change	• mental independence • developing moral sense (right and wrong) and exploring how things work and relate • moves from concrete to abstract learning • mode of learning through imagination • collaborates in small groups • less growth, more stable period	• social independence • developing social policy (how they would change the world) • sharing ideas and ideals with others • enormous physical and psychological change (similarities to the first plane)	• spiritual and moral independence • gives back to society • reasoning, logical mind • more stable period (similarities to the second plane)

IT'S TIME FOR A CHANGE IN EDUCATION

When we become parents, we begin to realize how the current education system is failing our children. We see an educational system that was built for the Industrial Revolution to train factory workers, where children sit in rows and memorize facts to pass tests.

You may be reading this book because you want to raise your children to be able to think for themselves, research to find answers to their questions, think creatively, be able to problem solve, work with others, and have meaning in their work.

People like Sir Ken Robinson, an educational and creativity expert, are constantly asking us to question the education system. To see that traditional schools kill creativity. To see that we need a revolution in the way our children learn.

I was just like you. I had a toddler and a baby, and I looked at the schooling options ahead. I was idealistic. I didn't want my children to learn just so they would pass tests. I walked into the Montessori classroom and saw there could be another way to learn.

IT'S TIME FOR PEACE

> "You have very truly remarked that if we are to teach real peace in this world, and if we are to carry on a real war against war, we shall have to begin with children and if they will grow up in their natural innocence, we won't have to struggle, we won't have to pass fruitless idle resolutions, but we shall go from love to love and peace to peace, until at last all the corners of the world are covered with that peace and love for which, consciously or unconsciously, the whole world is hungering."
>
> —Mahatma Gandhi, *Towards New Education*

It's time to take this information to the next level. I want to ask you to help me with my not-so-surreptitious plan to spread some peace and positivity in the world.

Often we feel helpless and like there is nothing we can do about all the violence in the world around us. But there is something we can do. We can learn to understand our toddlers better.

Once we can apply these principles with our toddlers, we can start spreading peace around us with our partners and our families, at school, in the supermarket, with friends, with strangers, and—most importantly—with people who see the world differently.

Let's apply the perspective-taking skills we have learned in this book. Let's sit in conversation, listen to each other, and really see each other.

We may have different approaches to raising our children and make different educational choices. We may have differences of sex, race, ethnicity, politics, sexuality, religion, and more. All our underlying beliefs and value systems may be different.

I truly believe that who is right is not important. What is important is for us to give significance to others, to give them belonging, and to accept them for who they are, just as we have learned to do with our toddlers. Our toddlers are enough, we are enough, and so is every living thing.

To come to peace in this world is to celebrate our differences, seek the commonalities, address others' fears, find peaceful ways to live together, and recognize that **we are more alike than we are different**. After all, we are all human.

So where can we start? With understanding our toddlers better. And planting the seeds to raise beautiful, curious, and responsible human beings.

Dr. Montessori died on May 6, 1952, in Noordwijk aan Zee, in the Netherlands. The inscription on her tomb says

> "I beg the dear all-powerful children to unite with me for the building of peace in Man and in the World."

TO PRACTICE

1. How can we prepare ourselves and our child as they grow from toddler to preschooler and beyond?
2. How can we apply the perspective-taking skills learned in this book to our relationships with:
   - our toddler?
   - our partner?
   - our family and friends?
   - neighbors?
   - strangers?
   - people who see the world differently?

REAL STORIES

HOME TOURS AND QUOTES FROM MONTESSORI FAMILIES

AUSTRALIA

Kylie, Aaron, Caspar, Otis, and Otto

How We Montessori

"No matter how much you read, I always recommend parents attend a Montessori parent-child class and experience Montessori in person."

"He is still very hands-on with his learning. I love to observe him in his element. He loves to bake sweets, and he gets so much enjoyment from cooking for his family. He loves getting messy with his art, and he loves being around his family. He is still very snuggly, and we love to curl up together with a good book."

"The thing that resonates the most about the Montessori approach is the way parents are taught to observe and follow the child. That each child learns at their own pace. This is magic."

MONGOLIA

Enerel, Bayanaa, Nimo, and Odi

Mininimoo

"I felt like my eyes were opened like never before when I saw the word *Montessori*. I could not sleep that day; I searched about it for the whole night and started preparing Montessori activities for my son the next day."

"I think teaching about discipline is much more important than the activities. Parents should set an example. We, as parents, also gain discipline throughout the process. And learn from the child. This takes a great amount of effort, but we get so much joy when the child is interested and learning."

"Even though my home and our Montessori room is small, I like to make it appear bigger, living in a small apartment. I try to squeeze everything in together and I make fewer items available at a given time. Always make a space for the child to explore. And I would suggest to try to always make a place cozy and comfortable."

CANADA

Beth, Anthony, and Quentin

Our Montessori Life

"Our absolute favorite thing to do is to be in nature with our boys, introducing them to all the natural world has to offer. So much natural learning happens when outside."

"We looked for a way to help our child meet his needs, on a holistic, individual level. Of course Montessori was the perfect and gentle answer."

"Above all, Montessori has at its center peace education. It is a pedagogy that has at its foundation the teaching of peace for the next generations. No other pedagogy or learning system has this. It's why I love Montessori so much."

"Montessori at home is about honoring and respecting the child. Can your child make their own food? Can they get their own clothes out of the closet? Do they have access to water or do you have to get them a drink? Most importantly, how do you speak to your children and the other members of your family?"

USA

Amy, James, Charlotte, and Simon

Midwest Montessori

"My favorite thing to do with my toddlers is observe them. Once I have prepared their environment, I absolutely love just sitting back and watching them at work. Through this, I have a glimpse into their minds, and it so fascinates me. Aside from watching them, I love spending time with them outdoors (either in nature or on the streets or in parks), reading books, listening and making music, and all things practical life."

"There is such care and detail placed upon creating an optimum environment for children to grow. This includes the preparation of the adult, which may be the most difficult part, particularly for a parent. We honor our children when we prepare ourselves and their home this way. The rest is up to them."

"We often think of toddlers as rambunctious, but if we take time to slow down, give them space, and observe, I have seen that young children can become deeply concentrated in their work."

MY FAMILY

Simone, Oliver, and Emma

Australia and the Netherlands

"View the world from the child's perspective. When we see the world through their eyes, we gain so much understanding and respect. And this will help you guide and support the child."

"I wanted my children to love learning, not to just pass tests. When we walked into a Montessori preschool, I was so touched. The thought that had been put into the activities laid out on the shelves. Everything was so beautiful. I wanted to start exploring everything myself, so I knew it was the right environment for my children."

"I'm constantly inspired as my own understanding of the Montessori philosophy deepens. It's like layers of an onion and you can just keep peeling back layer after layer. You can look at Montessori as just an approach to learning at school. But I love how Montessori can also be a way of life."

MY CLASSROOM

Jacaranda Tree Montessori

Amsterdam, the Netherlands

"Every week I welcome over 100 children with their parents and carers to learn in a Montessori environment, offering classes for babies, toddlers, and preschoolers."

"The children love to explore the environment, set up exactly for their age with everything accessible for them. The adults learn to observe the children, ask questions, and meet like-minded families. I love seeing both the children and the adults undergoing enormous transformation through coming to class."

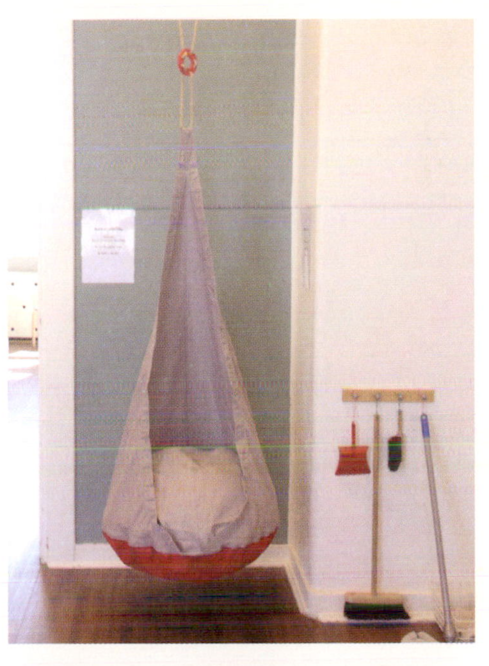

FURTHER READING

BOOKS AND LECTURES BY DR. MONTESSORI

The Absorbent Mind, Maria Montessori, Holt Paperbacks, 1995
The Child in the Family, Maria Montessori, ABC-CLIO, 1989
Education for a New World, Maria Montessori, ABC-CLIO, 1989
The Formation of Man, Maria Montessori, Association Montessori Internationale, 2007
The Secret of Childhood, Maria Montessori, Fides Publishers, 1966
The Discovery of the Child, Maria Montessori, Ballantine Books, 1986
Maria Montessori Speaks to Parents, Maria Montessori, Montessori-Pierson Publishing Company, 2017
The 1946 London Lectures, Maria Montessori, Montessori-Pierson Publishing Company, 2012

BOOKS ABOUT THE MONTESSORI APPROACH

The Joyful Child: Montessori, Global Wisdom for Birth to Three, Susan Mayclin Stephenson, Michael Olaf Montessori Company, 2013
Child of the World: Montessori, Global Education for Age 3-12+, Susan Mayclin Stephenson, Michael Olaf Montessori Company, 2013
Understanding the Human Being, Silvana Quattrocchi Montanaro M.D., Nienhuis Montessori, 1991
How to Raise an Amazing Child: The Montessori Way to Bring Up Caring, Confident Children, Tim Seldin, Dorling Kindersley, 2007
Maria Montessori: Her Life and Work, E. M. Standing, Plume, 1998
Montessori Madness, Trevor Eissler, Sevenoff, 2009
Montessori from the Start, Paula Polk Lillard and Lynn Lillard Jessen, Schocken, 2003

BOOKS ABOUT PARENTING

Positive Discipline: The First Three Years, Jane Nelsen, Ed. D., Three Rivers Press, 2007

How to Talk So Kids Will Listen and Listen So Kids Will Talk, Adele Faber and Elaine Mazlish, Piccadilly Press, 2013

Siblings Without Rivalry, Adele Faber and Elaine Mazlish, W. W. Norton & Company, 2012

The Whole-Brain Child: 12 Proven Strategies to Nurture Your Child's Developing Mind, Daniel J. Siegel, MD, and Tina Payne Bryson, MD, Delacorte, 2012

Unconditional Parenting: Moving from Rewards and Punishments to Love and Reason, Alfie Kohn, Atria Books, 2006

The Sleep Lady's Good Night, Sleep Tight, Kim West, Vanguard Press, 2010

Thriving!: Raising Confident Kids with Confidence, Character and Resilience, Michael Grose, Bantam, 2010

Toxic Childhood: How the Modern World Is Damaging Our Children and What We Can Do About It, Sue Palmer, Orion, 2006

The Creative Family Manifesto: How to Encourage Imagination and Nurture Family Connections, Amanda Soule, Roost Books, 2008

A Parents' and Teachers' Guide to Bilingualism, Colin Baker, Multilingual Matters, 2014

BOOKS ON PERSONAL DEVELOPMENT

Nonviolent Communication, Marshall B. Rosenberg, Phd, Puddledancer Press, 2003

Mindset: How We Can Learn to Fulfill Our Potential, Carol S. Dweck, Ballantine Books, 2007

Quiet: The Power of Introverts in a World That Can't Stop Talking, Susan Cain, Penguin Books, 2012

In Praise of Slow: How a Worldwide Movement Is Challenging the Cult of Speed, Carl Honoré, Orion, 2005

The Five Love Languages, Gary Chapman, Northfield Publishing, 2004

OTHER RESOURCES

"Seeing Tantrums as Distress, Not Defiance," Jenny Anderson, the *New York Times*, October 30, 2011

"Lexical Development in Bilingual Infants and Toddlers: Comparison to Monolingual Norms," Barbara Pearson et al., *Language Learning* 43, no. 1 (March 1993), 93–120

Sarah Ockwell-Smith, https://sarahockwell-smith.com/2015/03/19/one-simple-way-to-improve-your-baby-or-child-sleep/

Yoram Mosenzon, Connecting2Life, www.connecting2life.net/

Screen-Free Parenting, www.screenfreeparenting.com

Scilla Elworthy, www.scillaelworthy.com

Sir Ken Robinson, www.sirkenrobinson.com

Rusty Keeler, www.earthplay.net

THANK-YOUS

I have so much gratitude and appreciation for . . .

HIYOKO—I could not have asked for a more amazing illustrator for this project. I never could have dreamed that this book could be so beautiful. I would send an idea to Hiyoko to include in the book and it always came back exactly as I meant and even better than I expected. Her aesthetic, care, and generosity are of the highest quality. Thank you, Hiyoko, for translating my words into this beautifully illustrated and designed book.

ALEXIS—What a pleasure and honor to have Alexis and her brain working on this book with me. I asked Alexis to help me with a bit of copy editing. It turned into her giving me feedback on every word in this book. Her light and sensitive touch made the manuscript even better.

THE TEAM AT WORKMAN PUBLISHING—I'm still reeling in happiness that Workman has taken on this book to help me with my not-so-surreptitious plan to spread some peace and positivity around the world. Special thanks to Page for finding this book and bringing it to Workman; to Maisie for all your hours of work, staying forever positive, being an amazing editor, and listening to all my requests; to Rebecca, Lathea, Moira, and Cindy for getting the word out in fun and creative ways; to Galen for all his book layout skills and for appeasing the many design requests; to Kristina for getting this book into more and more countries; to Sun for the super organizational skills; and to the rest of the team at Workman working behind the scenes.

EXTRA HELPERS—Dyana, Kevin, and Niina were so kind as to be early readers and gave generous feedback on the book. Lucy and Tania also read through it to dot the "i's" and cross the "t's." Yoram generously contributed the feelings and needs table in the appendix. And Maddie jumped in to do some invaluable quote research, too. For the Montessori quotes, I was inundated with help from my Montessori friends who had fun tracking down all the sources for Dr. Montessori's wisdom. Thank you all for your invaluable help to make this book the best it could possibly be.

FAMILIES FOR SHARING THEIR HOMES—I am constantly surprised by the generosity and kindness of others. When I reached out to the families whose homes and children are featured in this book, they unhesitatingly offered to share their photos and lives with us. I hope you find their stories and photos pure inspiration for bringing Montessori into your own home. Thank you to Anna, Kylie, Enerel, Beth, and Amy for sharing the beauty, the joy, and the calm that Montessori has brought to your families.

MY INSPIRATION—I am eternally grateful for being introduced to Montessori by these three wise ladies—Ferne Van Zyl, An Morison, and Annabel Needs. I was lucky enough to attend classes with my children and work with Ferne, getting an amazing introduction to Montessori. Ferne shared her love for Montessori with me and showed me how to see things from the child's perspective. An and Annabel were my children's first Montessori teachers. It was from attending an open day at Castlecrag Montessori School in Sydney, Australia, that I was first touched by the beauty of a Montessori classroom, the respect of Montessori teachers, and the care with which everything is prepared for the children. Thank you for inspiring me to follow in your footsteps.

MY MONTESSORI TRAINER—Judi Orion shared her love of babies and toddlers with us and her wealth of experience during our AMI Assistants to Infancy training. I soaked up every word of our training and found the training so thorough in preparing us for all the work we do with children. A fundamental part of the training that I learned from Judi was the power of observation—learning to see the child with fresh eyes every day and accepting them for who they are. Thank you Judi for showing me how to see in a new way.

MONTESSORI FRIENDS—I have had the pleasure of learning from many Montessori friends both in person and online. These include Heidi Phillipart-Alcock, Jeanne-Marie Paynel, the lovely folk in the AMI head office, Eve Hermann and family, Pamela Green and Andy Lulka, and all the Montessori community from the Montessori congresses to our online

Montessori communities. Thank you for sharing your wisdom and helping me to keep growing and learning every day.

FAMILIES AT JACARANDA TREE MONTESSORI—I feel very grateful to work with such amazing families who come to my classes at Jacaranda Tree Montessori here in Amsterdam. Every week I greet more than 100 children and their mamas, papas, carers, grandparents, and others. I am learning from these families every day.

MY MUM + DAD + SISTERS—and all my extended family. We are a funny, random bunch. So different from each other in many ways, but so similar in others. My parents have always supported me, even when I say, "I think I'm going to be a Montessori teacher" or "move 16,633 kilometers away." I love chatting with them all on Sunday mornings and catching up on each other's news. Thank you for giving me both roots and wings.

LUKE—for dreaming about having kids while wandering through the market in London that day and for making it a reality. For working the night shift and waking up to look after Oliver and Emma while I did my Montessori training. For living in the UK, Australia, and the Netherlands. For all I have learned through 17 years of marriage, through separating amicably, and through our ongoing co-parenting journey. I would not have wanted to do it with anyone else. Thank you for being my intellectual sparring partner.

MY WORK BUDDY—When we work for ourselves, it can be hard to find the support we need. And then one day there was Debbie. She is not just my weekly work buddy. She listened to me go through a huge transition, we went on work retreats in cabins, had nature adventures with our children, and her family are the best people to share Sint "surprises" with. Then we wrote our books side by side at the cafe, celebrating and supporting each other. She is always there with a listening ear and just the right words. Thank you for Thursday afternoon work sessions and more.

MY FRIENDS—I have friends here in Amsterdam who hear all the nitty gritty as we catch up over coffee, stroll around a museum, or see a film. I have old friends whom I speak to less often but pick up exactly where we leave off and seem to be flowing in the same path even if we aren't in the same city. Thank you Rachel, Agi, Michelle, Birgit, Emily, Becci, Narelle, Emmy, Claire, Monika, and many others for all the fun to fuel my work.

KICKSTARTER BACKERS—I am indebted to all the people who backed this book in its early Kickstarter days, and for trusting me and helping to get this project off the ground and into homes all around the world.

ALL THE THINGS—for everything around me, from the cups of tea, to the nature visits, to cycling on my bike to class, to my bath, to yoga in the living room, to cozy spots where I've perched with my laptop to write this book (cafes, sitting outside, my bed, my kitchen table, my desk, the couch, a train through France, a plane to Stockholm, an apartment in Lyon), to my camera for capturing the beauty around me, to the internet for allowing me to connect with so many people, to the inspiring podcasts, to ALL the books, to Amsterdam which I now call home. I have so much I am grateful for.

TO YOU—for joining me in this work to spread peace in the world, one family at a time. Thank you, thank you, thank you.

MY OWN CHILDREN—Lastly, I want to thank the most important people in my life, Oliver and Emma. They are my favorite people to spend time with. They have taught me so much about being a parent, and I have loved growing up alongside them. Their support, patience, and understanding for my work means so much to me. Thank you from the bottom of my heart both for being you and for putting up with me talking nonstop about this project. Thank you for the pure love that fills my heart to write this book.

APPENDIX

INSTEAD OF THIS, SAY THAT

TO...	INSTEAD OF THIS...	SAY THAT...
See through our child's eyes	Denying: "Don't worry about it. It's just a bump."	See the situation from their perspective/ acknowledge their feelings: "Was that a shock? A bump can hurt."
	Judging: "You are always taking toys from other children."	Translate for them: "It sounds like you would like to have a turn when they are all finished."
	Blaming, lecturing: "You shouldn't have..." "What you should do is..."	Seek to understand by guessing how they feel: "Are you telling me...?" "It looks like you..." "Are you feeling...?" "It seems like..."
Build independence	Telling them what not to do: "Don't drop the glass!"	Tell them how to have success: "Use two hands."
	Avoid always taking the lead: "Let's go take a look at the puzzles."	Follow the child: Say nothing (wait to see what they choose).
Help our child	Taking over and doing it for them: "Let me do it for you..."	Step in as little as possible and as much as necessary: "Would you like me/someone to help you?" "Would you like to see how I do it?" "Have you tried...?"
Help our child love learning	Correcting: "No, it's an elephant."	Teach by teaching: "Ah. You wanted to show me the rhinoceros." (Then make a note to teach them *elephant* at another time.)
Cultivate curiosity	Giving the answers to all questions: "The sky is blue because..."	Encourage them to find out: "I don't know. Let's find out together."
Help our child assess for themselves, i.e., cultivate intrinsic motivation	Praising: "Good job!" "Good boy/girl!"	1. Give feedback, describe effort: "You put all the trucks in the basket." 2. Sum it up with a word: "Now, that's what I call being resourceful." 3. Describe how we feel: "It's a pleasure to walk into a tidy room."
Share	Forcing them to share: "Give them a turn now."	Allow them to finish and share by taking turns: "It looks like they are playing with it right now. It will be available soon."
Accept our child for who they are	Dismissing their angry/big feelings: "It's just a spoon. Don't be silly."	Acknowledge and allow all feelings: "It looks like you are upset that your favorite spoon isn't available."
Remind them of a house/ground rule	Shouting: "No fighting!"	Have a few house rules: "I can't let you hurt them. Use your words to tell them what you would like."
Cultivate cooperation	Saying no: "Don't touch the baby!"	Use positive language: "We are gentle with the baby."

TO . . .	INSTEAD OF THIS . . .	SAY THAT . . .
	Getting involved in the problem: "You are driving me crazy. Why don't you get dressed? We need to leave!"	Find ways to solve the problem: "How can we find a way to solve the problem? Let's make a checklist of all the things we need to do to leave in the morning."
	Getting frustrated: "Why don't you listen to me? It's bath time!"	Find ways to involve the child: "Would you like to hop to the bath like a rabbit or walk sideways on all fours like a crab?"
	Nagging, shouting: "How many times do I have to ask you to put your shoes on?"	Use one word: "Shoes."
	Repeating ourselves: "Don't go near the oven again!"	Write a note: "The sign says, 'It's hot.'"
	Accusing: "Why don't you ever put away your toys when you are finished?"	Show them: "It goes here" (while tapping the shelf).
Help our child be responsible	Threatening, punishing, bribing, or giving a time-out: "If you do that again, I'll . . ." "If you come now, I'll give you a sticker." "Go to time-out to think about what you have done!"	Help them calm down and then make amends: "You look upset. Would you like a cuddle?" "Would you like to go to your calm place to calm down?" *THEN* "Our friend is crying. How can we make it up to them?"
Communicate limits	Avoiding conflict, being very strict, or setting a bad example: "They are too young to know what they are doing." "If you bite me again, I'll bite you and let you see if you like it."	Set a kind and clear limit: "I can't let you hit/throw/bite me. I'm going to put you down. If you need to bite, you can bite on this apple."
Avoid sibling rivalry	Comparing siblings: "Why don't you eat your peas like your sister/brother?"	Treat each child uniquely: "It sounds like you would like some more."
	Putting the eldest in charge: "You are a big brother/sister now. You should know better."	Give all siblings responsibility: "Can you both look after each other while I visit the bathroom?"
Be neutral in sibling disputes	Trying to decide who is right and wrong: "What happened here?"	Leave them to solve the problem: "I see two kids who want the same toy. I know you can come up with a solution that both of you are happy with."
Avoid using roles and labels	Putting a child in a role or using labels: "They are the shy one/the clever one."	Give them another view of themselves: "I noticed that you asked for help all by yourself."
Communicate with family/other caregivers	Getting angry with a family member: "Why are you shouting at them?"	Translate for them: "It sounds like Mom/Dad would like you to . . ."
Model grace and courtesy	Blaming others: "You should have told me earlier."	Take responsibility: "What I should have done is . . ." "What I should have said is . . ."

WHERE TO FIND MONTESSORI MATERIALS AND FURNITURE

Sources for materials and furniture will vary from country to country. However, here are some suggestions of places to get started.

I like to recommend first looking locally where possible to support local businesses and to reduce our footprint by minimizing shipping costs.

A few things from somewhere like Ikea can be useful for basics, and we can customize them to add our own unique touch. They have some suitable low shelving, tables and chairs, arts and crafts materials, book ledges, and items for the hallway, kitchen, and bathroom.

1. Activities

To find a wide selection of wooden puzzles; sorting, stacking, posting, and threading activities; and musical instruments, look in wooden-toy shops or secondhand stores.

Coin boxes can be found at stationery shops or specialty lock shops.

Another activity that is easy to set up at home is a basket full of purses with hidden treasures inside. I love finding these purses at flea markets and thrift stores. Some favorite hidden treasures to look for are small spinning tops, miniature animals, a small toy baby, and trinkets found on key chains (with the key chain removed). (As these items are often small and possible choking hazards, always offer with supervision.)

I also love Schleich plastic animals; they are a bit expensive but great for gifts. They're available at wooden-toy shops or online.

2. Craft Supplies

For small scissors; painting supplies; chunky, good-quality pencils; and watercolor paints, look in an art supply shop. There we can also find paper and paintbrushes in various sizes.

3. Baskets and Trays

Baskets and trays are perfect for organizing the activities on our shelves at home. We can look in storage supply shops, thrift shops, or department stores. Muji stores also have some lovely options.

4. Snack Area

Be on the hunt for a kitchen or housewares store that stocks glasses that are the right size for small hands while being durable and chip resistant. Look for glass, not plastic. We show the child how to use real objects around the home. If they are aware that the items may break, they learn to carry these items with care. Drinking from a glass tastes better, is a more sustainable choice, and doesn't tip over as easily when our child is learning to pour a drink for themselves. I use the smallest size of Duralex glasses in my classroom.

We can find nice enamel bowls in housewares shops or small metal bowls at Ikea, as well as cute tin boxes for crackers in antiques stores or at Ikea.

5. Cleaning

We can also include small cleaning items in our kitchen area, such as a mop, broom, or dustpan with brush. These are generally available at toy shops or online. Hand mitts (made of terry cloth to fit over the hand) are useful to have at the ready; look in department stores. I have found some great toddler-sized aprons on Etsy by searching "Montessori aprons."

6. Furniture

We may be able to find a workshop where they can make us a small table, chair, and low shelves. I also like to look at secondhand shops. The shelves in our class are 47 inches long by 12 inches deep by 16 inches high (120 cm by 30 cm by 40 cm).

ABOUT MONTESSORI SCHOOLS

What to look for in a Montessori school

Because the name *Montessori* was never copyrighted, there is a wide range of so-called Montessori schools, and it can be difficult to know which are genuinely applying the principles and theories of Dr. Montessori.

Here are ten things to look for:

1. The school promotes hands-on understanding of the world with tangible materials. The children make discoveries for themselves through touching, exploring, and working with beautiful, solid materials.

2. The materials are set out on shelves at the children's level. The activities are beautiful, attractively presented on trays or in baskets, with no missing parts.

3. There are mixed age groups: 3-to-6-year-olds, 6-to-9-year-olds, and 9-to-12-year-olds. The older children can model for, and help, the younger children.

4. The work time is unstructured. The children are free to choose what they work on and free to work uninterrupted for (ideally) three-hour periods.

5. The children are happy and independent.

6. There is little or no testing. The teacher knows which activities each child has mastered, so there is little need to test a child.

7. The teacher has completed a recognized Montessori training program. I particularly like Association Montessori Internationale, because this is the training organization Dr. Montessori's family set up to maintain the integrity of their courses.

8. The teacher talks respectfully to the children as a guide, encouraging them to be resourceful about finding answers to their questions: "I don't know. Let's find out!"

9. Natural learning is emphasized over traditional learning. Rather than the teacher standing at the front of the class telling the children what they need to know, the children are free to explore and make discoveries for themselves in a natural way.

10. The school treats each child as a unique individual, while looking at all aspects of their development (social, emotional, physical, cognitive, and linguistic).

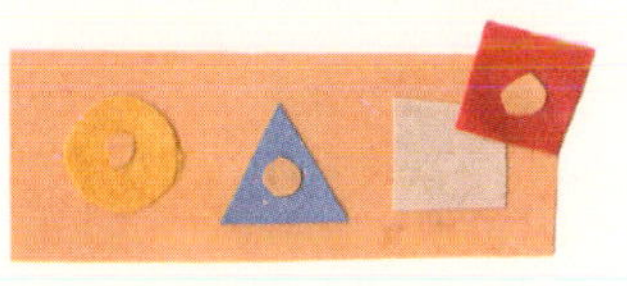

What does a typical day at a Montessori school look like?

It can be difficult for parents to understand how there can be thirty children in a Montessori class, all working on different lessons and on different subjects simultaneously. I often get asked, "How can the teacher manage all this?"

Here's an impression of how it works in practice.

Before the day starts, the Montessori teacher has prepared the classroom. Activities line the shelves at the children's height in the various subject areas, with meticulously arranged materials that scaffold onto each other, building skills upon skills upon skills. During the class, the teacher observes the children, sees what each child is learning and mastering, and offers the next lesson to a child when they are ready.

If we walk into a Montessori classroom, we might see one child working on their math skills, another child doing a language activity, and an additional pair of children completing a project together. The idea is that the child can choose for themselves what they would like to work on.

In a Montessori classroom, less time is spent on "crowd control," such as getting everyone to sit and listen to a lesson or visiting the bathroom as a group. This gives the teacher more time to focus on observing and helping the children.

Because the children in the classroom are in mixed-age groups, older children can help younger children. When they explain something to another child, they consolidate their own learning. The younger children also learn from observing older children.

We might be concerned that, with all this freedom, our child might avoid an area of learning. If this happens, the Montessori teacher will observe whether the child is not yet ready, and they can offer them activities that may be more accessible and attractive to them, showing them in a different way that follows their interests.

Is Montessori suitable for every child?

We often wonder if Montessori is suitable for all children or only for children who can plan well, are very independent, or can sit quietly to work.

1. Does Montessori work for different learning types?

I've found that Montessori is suitable for all children. The materials offer opportunities to learn visually, aurally, kinesthetically (through touch), and verbally, so they appeal to children who learn in different ways.

Some children learn by observing, others by doing. Children do not have to be "busy" all the time—they are welcome to observe others doing an activity. Sometimes, they will have learned so much through observation that by the time they try the same activity themselves, they are already close to mastering it. Another child may learn more by doing the activity themselves, repeating and repeating it until they master it. Both children can thrive in this environment, despite their different learning styles.

2. Does our child have to be able to plan?

Planning their day is something Montessori children learn how to do over time. In younger age groups, children follow their natural rhythm and interests. As they get older, they gradually build their planning skills in small steps.

Some children may need more guidance than others. A trained Montessori teacher should be able to guide children who need more assistance with organizing their work.

3. What if our child needs to move a lot?

A Montessori approach can be ideal for children who need to move. When we enter a Montessori classroom, it can often seem surprisingly quiet. The children appear focused on their activities without the teacher having to yell at them to calm down.

However, we also notice that the children are free to move around the classroom, observe others, and go to the toilet when necessary. In addition, a lot of movement is built into the activities themselves, so Montessori can be perfect for a child who needs to move.

4. Does Montessori match our parenting approach at home?

Montessori is suitable for all children, but some may find the limits of the classroom too constraining, and others may find the freedoms of the classroom too permissive.

I believe that Montessori works best when the child experiences a similar approach at home, where parents respect the child but also set clear limits—and the child learns to stay within them.

How does a child transition to a traditional school after being at Montessori?

Parents are often concerned that their child may need to switch to a traditional school at some stage in the future.

It is natural to think, *How will my child adjust to having to listen to the teacher giving the same lesson to everyone? To follow the teacher's timeline, rather than my child's? To sit still during class?*

Children generally transition well from Montessori schools to other schools. They are usually very independent, respectful, and sensitive to the other children—skills that are useful as they move to a new school.

I've heard a child say about the transition, "It's easy. You just have to do what the teacher tells you."

In another case, a child had been in Montessori schools until high school. The biggest challenges she faced were:
1. Asking the teacher if she could use the toilet
2. Not being able to look up information during tests if she didn't know the answer, because she was used to finding out the solution herself

Another family found it amusing that the children in the new school always put up their hands to ask the teacher if something was on the test. The Montessori children were used to learning because they loved to do so, not because they were being tested.

FEELINGS AND NEEDS

I have learned a lot from the Nonviolent Communication courses run by Yoram Mosenzon from connecting2life.net. I asked him if I could include his feelings and needs tables in this book, and he kindly agreed.

PLEASANT (EXPANSION) — **FEELINGS • SENSATIONS • EMOTIONS** — **UNPLEASANT (CONSTRICTION)**

CALM
relaxed, serene, tranquil, peaceful, quiet, at ease, comfortable, trusting, relieved, centered, content, fulfilled, satisfied, mellow

HAPPY
amused, animated, delighted, glad, joyful, pleased

CURIOUS
fascinated, interested, involved, engaged, inspired

REFRESHED
rested, enlivened, restored, reactivated, clearheaded

LIVELY
excited, enthusiastic, eager, energetic, passionate, vibrant, anticipation, blissful, ecstatic, radiant, thrilled, astonished, amazed, optimistic

COMPASSION
tender, warm, openhearted, loving, affection, friendly, sympathetic, touched

GRATEFUL
appreciative, thankful, moved, encouraged

CONFIDENT
empowered, open, proud, safe, hopeful

CONFUSED
torn, lost, hesitant, baffled, perplexed, puzzled

FEAR
afraid, scared, suspicious, panicked, paralyzed, terrified, apprehensive

VULNERABLE
fragile, insecure, reserved, sensitive

JEALOUS
envious

FATIGUE
overwhelmed, burnout, exhausted, sleepy, tired

BODY SENSATIONS
pain, tense, shaky, breathless, squeezed, shrink, sick, weak, empty, choked

UNCOMFORTABLE
troubled, unsettled, restless, uncertain, disquiet, agitated, disturbed, cranky, shocked, surprised, alert, uneasy

SAD
heavy hearted, disappointed, discouraged, melancholy, depressed, gloomy, pity, longing, despair, helpless, hopeless, nostalgic

PAIN
hurt, heartbroken, lonely, miserable, suffer, grief, agony, devastated, regretful, remorseful, guilt, turmoil

ANNOYED
irritated, frustrated, impatient, displeased, exasperated, unsatisfied

WORRIED
concerned, stressed, nervous, anxious, edgy, unquiet

EMBARRASSED
ashamed, shy

BORED
disconnected, alienated, apathetic, cold, numb, withdrawn, impatient

ANGRY
upset, furious, rage, resentful

HATE
dislike, hostile, aversion, bitter, disgusted, scorn

How to use these tables: When we have a thought, we can use the "Feelings/Sensations/Emotions" table to pinpoint what we are actually feeling. Once we've identified the feeling, we can use the table of "Universal Basic Needs" to see which underlying need is not being met, for example, to be seen or heard. Then, we are able to be more compassionate with ourselves and communicate more effectively with others about our feelings. We can also turn this compassion to others and try to understand their feelings and needs.

UNIVERSAL BASIC NEEDS

PHYSICAL WELL-BEING

air
nourishment (food, water)
light
warmth
rest / sleep
movement / physical exercise
health
touch
sexual expression
shelter / security / protection / safety / protection from pain / emotional safety / preservation
comfort

HARMONY

peace
beauty
order
calm / relaxation / equanimity / tranquility
stability / balance
ease
communion / wholeness
completion / digestion / integration
predictability / familiarity
equality / justice / fairness

CONNECTION

love
belonging
closeness
intimacy
empathy / compassion
appreciation
acceptance
recognition
reassurance
affection
openness
trust
communication
sharing / exchange
giving / receiving
attention
tenderness / softness
sensitivity / kindness
respect
seeing (see / be seen)
hearing (hear / be heard)
understanding (understand / be understood)
consideration / care / that my needs matter
inclusion / participation
support / help / nurturing
cooperation / collaboration
community / companionship / partnership / fellowship
mutuality / reciprocity
consistency / continuity

MEANING

purpose
contribution / enrich life
centeredness
hope / faith
clarity
to know (be in reality)
learning
awareness / consciousness
inspiration / creativity
challenge / stimulation
growth / evolution / progress
empowerment / power / having inner strength / competence / capacity
self-value / self-confidence / self-esteem / dignity
efficacy / effectiveness
liberation / transformation
to matter / take part in / have my place in the world
spirituality
interdependence
simplicity
celebration / mourning

FREEDOM

choice / acting out of my own spirituality
autonomy
independence
space / time

HONESTY

self-expression
authenticity
integrity
transparency
realness / truth

PLAY

liveliness / alive / vitality
flow
passion
spontaneity
fun
humor / laugh / lightness
discovery / adventure
variety / diversity

Note: The words in this list are not "pseudo feelings," like when we say we are feeling "attacked." Pseudo feelings often imply the person receiving our message is at fault. So stick to words on this list that have been carefully selected so that we will be heard.

PLAY-DOUGH RECIPE

To make the best play dough, you usually have to cook it, which gets very messy. This recipe uses boiling water instead. We just stir the ingredients, add the boiling water, mix for a few minutes until it's cool, then knead. Voilà, we've got lovely play dough.

INGREDIENTS (makes about a cup [240 ml] of play dough)

Regular Play Dough

1 cup (125 g) flour

2 tablespoons cream of tartar

½ cup (150 g) salt

¾ to 1 cup (175 to 250 ml) boiling water

1 tablespoon cooking oil

Food coloring or cinnamon, spirulina powder, or other natural coloring

Chocolate Mud Play Dough

1¼ cups (150 g) flour

½ cup (50 g) cocoa

1 teaspoon cream of tartar

¼ cup (75 g) salt

¾ to 1 cup (175 to 250 ml) boiling water

2 tablespoons cooking oil

INSTRUCTIONS

1. The children can mix the dry ingredients together in a medium bowl.
2. Add the boiling water, food coloring, and oil to dry ingredients and mix until it pulls away from the edges of the bowl. (This is a step for the adult.)
3. Once the mixture is cool enough (this takes a few minutes), have the children knead it until it's smooth.
4. Store in sealed container for up to 6 months. Does not need to be refrigerated.

LIST OF MONTESSORI ACTIVITIES FOR TODDLERS

AGE	ACTIVITY NAME	DESCRIPTION/MATERIALS	AREA OF DEVELOPMENT
All ages	Music/dance/movement/singing	• Playing musical instruments • Listening to beautiful music (preferably not as background music but as the focus) • Dancing and moving to explore and stretch the body • Singing	• Music and movement
All ages	Books	• Collection of books with realistic images that relate to the life a young child is living • One picture per page for infant, *then* one picture with one word, *then* a picture with a sentence, *then* build to simple stories, and *then* more complex stories • Arranged so that children can see their covers and access them easily, perhaps in a small basket for a few books or on a small bookshelf • Start with board books and move on to hardcover and paperback	• Language
All ages	Rhythmic language	• Poetry, songs, rhyming ditties • Simple and not too long • Fairly realistic • Finger and body movements that go along with them. Examples: action rhymes, finger rhymes, haiku, pat-a-cake	• Language
All ages	Self-expression	• Moments during the day when the child wants to share something with the adult • For a nonverbal child, it can be sounds, expressions, or poking out their tongue. • A verbal child will use words, then phrases and sentences. • The adult needs to get down to the child's eye level, maintain eye contact (if culturally appropriate), and be present. • We can restate what they have said. • Through body language and speech, the adult lets the child know that we are very interested in what they are sharing.	• Language
12 months	Scribbling	• Block crayon or chunky pencil (like Stabilo 3 in 1) • Paper—different sizes, colors, textures • Underlay to protect entire table, or a place mat	• Art/self-expression
12 months	Easel-chalk	• Chalkboard—examples: 1. on the other side of a painting easel; 2. very large piece of plywood with chalkboard paint, wall mounted low to ground; and/or 3. small chalkboard that sits on a shelf • Chalk—start with white and gradually introduce colors and different types of chalk • Small eraser	• Art/self-expression
Able to stand unaided	Easel-paint	• Easel • Paper that completely covers surface of easel • Start with one color of thick paint in a cup and gradually introduce other colors one by one. Can use two or more colors for an older child. • Chunky paintbrush with short handle • Painting smock/apron • Cup hook to hang smock/apron • Paper rolled in bin • Wet cloth to wipe up spills	• Art/self-expression

AGE	ACTIVITY NAME	DESCRIPTION/MATERIALS	AREA OF DEVELOPMENT
12+ months	Base with rings of dimensional gradation	• Base with spindle and four or five rings of varying gradation, ideally alternating colors • Bottom ring should not be bigger than child's hand span.	• Activities for eye-hand coordination
12+ months	Nuts and bolts	• One- or two-shaped bolts with a corresponding nut of the same shape • Have the nut on the bolt to start	• Activities for eye-hand coordination
12+ months	Opening and closing	• Basket with two or three common household objects for opening and closing, for example, a decorative box, tin, purse with snap fastener, makeup containers, toothbrush holder	• Activities for eye-hand coordination
12+ months	Vocabulary objects	• Three to six real or replica objects from the same category • Examples: fruits, vegetables, clothing, zoo animals, farm animals, pets, insects, mammals, birds, vertebrates, invertebrates, and so on	• Aids language development • Expands vocabulary
12+ months	Peg box	• Wooden box with six holes along back and an inset tray area for placing pegs removed from holes	• Refinement of eye-hand coordination and grasp
12+ months	Cubes on a vertical dowel	• Base with three cubes on dowel—keep cubes in basket or on dowel • Preparation for bead stringing	• Refinement of eye-hand coordination and grasp
12–14+ months	Puzzles	• Collection of knobbed puzzles progressing through greater and greater degrees of difficulty • Subject matter depicted on puzzle needs to be realistic and appealing, for example, animals or construction vehicles.	• Refinement of eye-hand coordination and pincer grasp • Develops the ability to recognize a background shape
Around 13+ months	Locks and keys	• Lock with the key strongly attached to a string	• Activities for eye-hand coordination
Once a child can walk	Table wiping	• Tray or basket with a sponge/drying mitt • Replacement sponges/mitts	• Care of environment
14+ months	Objects with identical cards for matching	• Classified sets of objects that have matching cards • Pictures that are identical to objects—in size and color, if possible—where the object can be put on top so that it covers the picture completely	• Aids language development • Helps a child move from 3D object to a 2D representation
14+ months	Objects with similar cards for matching	• Classified sets of objects that have matching cards • Similar pictures of the objects, perhaps different in color, size, or other	• Aids language development • With similar cards, allows the child to extract the essence of the object
14+ months	Wooden box with sliding lid	• Box with sliding lid, object inside, changed regularly	• Refinement of eye-hand coordination and grasp
14+ months	Box with bins	• Wooden box with three bins that open out • Three different objects, placed in each bin	• Refinement of eye-hand coordination and grasp • To exercise the wrist motion

AGE	ACTIVITY NAME	DESCRIPTION/MATERIALS	AREA OF DEVELOPMENT
14+ months	Posting activities	• Boxes for posting different shapes and sizes • Basic set with a single shape, for example, one lid with a circle, one with a square, one with a triangle, and one with a rectangle • Make it more challenging—for example, two shapes cut out of one lid—and then even more challenging—for example, with four shapes	• Refinement of eye-hand coordination and grasp • Introduction to, and naming of, geometric solids
14+ months, walking steadily	Watering plants	• Tray (to protect shelf) • Small watering can • Small container with small piece of dish sponge • Plant	• Care of environment
14+ months	Undressing, dressing, and storing clothes	• Putting on and taking off their own coat, shoes, and clothing and hanging them on a hook or putting the items in a basket	• Care of self
14+ months	Handwashing at sink	• Bar of soap or liquid soap • Towel	• Care of self
14+ months	Wiping nose	• Tissues—can be cut in half and folded • Mirror • Small trash can with swinging lid • Show them how you wipe your own nose; then allow them to wipe their nose.	• Care of self
14+ months	Brushing teeth	• Bathroom sink • Place to store toothbrush • Toothbrush • Toothpaste • Allow child to start brushing their teeth; then, offer to finish for them.	• Care of self
14+ months	Dressing frame: Velcro	• Wooden frame, two pieces of fabric fastened with Velcro • To practice opening and closing Velcro	• Care of self
14–16 months	Climbing	• For example, dome climbers, poles, climbing wall, obstacle courses, trees	• Activities for gross-motor movement
14–16 months	Pushing/pulling	• For example, a wheelbarrow for pushing and a wagon for pulling	• Activities for gross-motor movement
14–16 months	Brachiating—swinging by arms like a monkey	• For example, monkey bars, rings	• Activities for gross-motor movement
14–16 months	Sliding	• Ideally with large platform at top and wide enough for them to manage independently	• Activities for gross-motor movement
14–16 months	Running	• For example, running tracks with arrows; a basket of balls sits at each end of the track and the child carries a ball from basket to basket	• Activities for gross-motor movement
14–16 months	Jumping	• For example, jumping over a line flat on the floor; once child is jumping with both feet, you can introduce something with elevation	• Activities for gross-motor movement
14–16 months	Riding	• For example, a balance bike or low trike propelled by pushing feet on floor; then from 2.5 years, you can introduce pedal tricycles	• Activities for gross-motor movement

AGE	ACTIVITY NAME	DESCRIPTION/MATERIALS	AREA OF DEVELOPMENT
14–16 months	Balancing	• Balance beam, for example, a plank of wood on top of some books or bricks • Initially walking sideways while holding on to wall/beam in front of them; then walking forward on beam holding on to wall with one hand; then one foot on beam, one foot on ground (and then alternate feet so other foot is on beam and so forth); then can alter height or move beam away from wall; can also crawl on a wide balance beam	• Activities for gross-motor movement
14–16 months	Swinging	• Ideally, low to ground so child can get on and off by themselves and push themselves. Child can lie over seat and push with feet or sit on seat, back up, then lift feet and go.	• Activities for gross-motor movement
14–16 months	Other movement possibilities	• Platform on semicircular base (aka therapy top or balance board)—very good for building balance, understanding feedback given by the body, and coordinating movement • Y-shaped tunnels made of natural elements like willow branches or similar • Labyrinths from box hedge • Sand pits • Ball or tire swing • Gardening and composting • Cave made out of natural elements, for example, sticks, willow, or similar • Running water	• Activities for gross-motor movement
14–16 months	Discs on horizontal dowel	• Straight, horizontal metal dowel on a wooden base with one to three discs	• Refinement of eye-hand coordination and grasp • To cross the midline • To work on wrist movements
14–16+ months	Discs on serpentine dowel	• Serpentine dowel made of metal on a wooden base with one to three discs	• Refinement of eye-hand coordination and grasp • To cross the midline • To work on wrist movements
Around 15–16+ months	Washing leaves	• Little (leaf-shaped) dish with sponge cut to size inside dish • Tray to protect shelf from water	• Care of environment
Around 15–18+ months	Latches	• Collection of latches attached to different furniture or doorways in a room, for example, latch with chain, hook latch, and bar latch	• Refinement of eye-hand coordination and grasp
Around 15–18+ months	Hair brushing	• Mirror plus hairbrush • Tray to carry hairbrush and a dish with hair clips and bands	• Care of self
Around 15–18+ months	Three pegs with small rings	• Wooden square base with three pegs in primary colors • Three rings of each color	• Refinement of eye-hand coordination and grasp

AGE	ACTIVITY NAME	DESCRIPTION/MATERIALS	AREA OF DEVELOPMENT
Around 16 to 18+ months	Clay	• Plastic mat or special table with canvas covering for clay work • Lump of real mud clay (white/terra-cotta) wrapped in a damp cloth in a container or white DAS clay or play dough or kinetic sand • Tools to sculpt and cut with	• Art/self-expression
16–18+ months	Sweeping	• Broom • A sweeping guide (or a circle drawn in chalk on the ground) can be used to show where to collect the dirt • Dustpan and brush	• Care of environment
16–18+ months	Dusting	• Dusting cloth	• Care of environment
16–18+ months	Mopping	• Child-sized mop or flat mop with washcloth attached • Hang mop on cleaning stand	• Care of environment
16–18+ months	Dusting plants	• Handmade plant duster made of wool • Container to hold duster	• Care of environment
16–18+ months	Dressing frame: zipper	• Wooden frame, two pieces of fabric fastened with a zipper • The fabric does not come apart—the zipper is attached at the bottom. • Metal ring can be placed on the zipper pull. • Practice using a zipper	• Care of self
16–18+ months	Bead stringing	• Piece of plastic tubing used as thread—easier to use initially because it allows the child to push a bit of thread through the bead • Five or six wooden beads—can build to more beads • More challenging: thicker string, bigger beads, a shoelace with small beads	• Refinement of eye-hand coordination and grasp • Two hands working together
18+ months	Flower arranging	• Collection of different vases • Doilies • Flowers—cut to length to be used • Tray with a lip • Small jug • Small funnel • Sponge • The child can pour water into the vase using the funnel, place the flower in the vase, and arrange the vase on a table or shelf with the doily underneath.	• Care of environment
18+ months	Hanging up cloths	• Wet items of laundry—napkins, hand mitts, washcloths, aprons • Clothesline • Clothespins	• Care of environment
18+ months	Collecting debris and placing it on the compost pile/ in the compost bin	• Debris • Child-sized rake, dustpan, and brush • Wheelbarrow • Compost pile/compost bin	• Care of environment • Outdoor environment

AGE	ACTIVITY NAME	DESCRIPTION/MATERIALS	AREA OF DEVELOPMENT
18+ months	Germinating seeds	• Seeds—Use a small glass jar with a picture of the type of plant on the outside. Choose seeds that will germinate quickly (peas, beans, corn, radishes, pumpkins, sunflowers). • Small pots made of clay, newspaper, or peat • Small gardening hand tools, including trowel and rake • Apron • Small tray with a little dish • Small gardening tray and jug on windowsill or near light source • Dirt from outside or, if necessary, a bag of dirt	• Care of environment
18+ months	Other activities to take care of the outdoor environment	• Sweeping • Raking • Digging • Scrubbing tiles, tables, and benches • Watering plants • Picking and caring for flowers • Planting a flower/vegetable/herb garden that then requires ongoing care	• Care of environment
18+ months (able to carry a jug)	Handwashing at table	• Small basin for washing hands • Jug • Soap dish with small piece of soap • Apron • Washcloth for drying hands • Mitt to dry table • Discard bucket for the dirty water • Suitable for child wanting to repeat handwashing at sink	• Care of self
18+ months	Cleaning shoes	• Mat • Brush with handle, or nail brush	• Care of self
18+ months	Setting table	• Help set table with a basket for cutlery • Help lay tablecloth • Help fold napkins • Help make warm washcloths	• Food preparation
18+ months	Help to clear table	• Wipe face with warm washcloth • Bring plate and cutlery to kitchen	• Food preparation
18+ months	Preparing crackers	• Small spreaders • Small container of butter, nut spread, hummus, or similar • Small box of crackers • Child spreads a small amount of spread onto cracker and sits to eat. • Can prepare standing or sitting	• Food preparation
18+ months	Squeezing orange juice	• Citrus press or squeezer—look for one that the child can use independently • Jug to collect juice • Glass for drinking • Child can squeeze orange and bring peel to (compost) bin or trash can	• Food preparation
18+ months	Cutting banana	• Banana prepared by cutting a slit at the top so child can peel off skin, strip by strip • Chopping board • Butter knife/nonserrated knife to cut banana • Child can bring peel to (compost) bin or trash can • Child can place in bowl to serve on table	• Food preparation

AGE	ACTIVITY NAME	DESCRIPTION/MATERIALS	AREA OF DEVELOPMENT
18+ months	Peeling and cutting apple	• Peeler • Apple cutter/corer • Cutting board • Child can peel apple by laying it on the board and peeling from top to bottom. • The apple cutter is pushed from top to bottom to divide the apple into eight segments and to remove the core. • Child can place in bowl to serve on table.	• Food preparation
18+ months	Pour a glass of water	• Access to a tap/small jug/water dispenser • Glass • Have a sponge and hand mitt ready for spills	• Food preparation
18+ months	Watercolor painting	• Tray • Watercolor tablet • Small jar with water • Brush • Cloth to wipe up spills • Underlay • Paper • Show child how to wet brush, put paint on brush, paint onto paper.	• Art/self-expression
18+ months	Sorting objects	• Dish with three sections and two different kinds of the same item, such as shells, nuts, seed pods, geometric shapes—four of each kind	• Works with refinement of tactile sense • Aids in classifying abilities
18+ months	Vocabulary cards	• Sets of classified cards that relate to the child's life • Start with simple classifications	• Aids language development • To increase vocabulary
18–22+ months	Dressing frame: buttons	• Wooden frame, two pieces of fabric attached with three large buttons • Vertical buttonhole • To practice buttoning	• Care of self
18–22+ months	Dressing frame: snap fasteners	• Wooden frame, two pieces of fabric with snap fasteners	• Care of self
18–22+ months	Table washing	• Tray with bowl, soap, brush, and sponge for scrubbing table	• Care of environment
18 months–2+ years	Mirror polishing	• Little container of nontoxic mirror polish • Rectangular sponge as an applicator • Finger mitt • Underlay to place items on	• Care of environment
18 months–2+ years	Wood polishing	• Container that is easy for the child to handle • Bottle of nontoxic polish, such as beeswax • Small dish • Finger mitt • Items to polish	• Care of environment
18 months–2+ years	Gluing	• Gluing box with space for brush, glue pot with small amount of glue, up to six large shapes, and paper to glue onto	• Refinement of eye-hand coordination and grasp • To teach the practical skill of gluing • Refine movement of fingers • Art/self-expression

AGE	ACTIVITY NAME	DESCRIPTION/MATERIALS	AREA OF DEVELOPMENT
Around 2+ years	Washing dishes	• Table with two tubs • Dish brush with small handle, or small sponge • Travel-sized bottle of dishwashing detergent with small amount of liquid • Jug—plastic and transparent; can put mark on jug to show desired water level • Apron • Drying mitt • Hand-drying cloth	• Food preparation
Around 2+ years	Drying dishes	• Lay the drying cloth on the table, place bowl or glass on cloth; fold cloth into the bowl or glass; press; unfold.	• Food preparation
Around 2+ years	Cleaning windows	• Spray bottle with 1 cup (240 ml) of water (vinegar optional) • Small squeegee • Piece of chamois or cloth	• Care of environment
Around 2+ years	Washing cloths	• Table with two tubs • Small scrub board • Bar of soap • Soap dish • Jug • Two plastic baskets on either side of table on floor • Apron • Drying mitt • Hand-drying cloth	• Care of environment
Around 2+ years	Use of scissors	• Pair of small scissors in a case • Handmade envelopes • Narrow strips of index card, slim enough to allow the child to cut across the strip in one snip	• Refinement of eye-hand coordination and grasp • To learn practical skill of cutting • To develop precise hand movements
Around 2+ years	Classified stereognostic bags (mystery bags)	• Attractive bag with five to eight related, unrelated, or paired objects • Bag you can't easily look into, so child feels around the object • Examples: 1. Cooking implements—child-sized spreader, cookie cutter, sieve, bamboo whisk, spatula 2. Bag of items from another country, such as a bag made out of a kimono containing Japanese items 3. Hair items 4. Gardening tools	• To aid in the development of the stereognostic sense • To increase vocabulary
Around 2 years—the child needs some spoken language	Questioning exercise	• Conversations that can occur throughout the day, such as while folding laundry or preparing food • Example: "Do you remember when we planted the basil and then it started growing?" "Where did we plant the basil seeds?" "What did we use to pick the basil?" • Done very naturally and conversationally	• To use vocabulary they are developing • To broaden child's thinking, help them abstract information from their experiences, and verbalize it • Builds self-confidence • Allows the adult to model language usage

AGE	ACTIVITY NAME	DESCRIPTION/MATERIALS	AREA OF DEVELOPMENT
2+ years	Sewing	• In a basket or box - Scissors - Thread - Needle case with blunt tapestry or embroidery needle - First sewing card consists of a punched diagonal line on a square card; progress to holes in square and circle shapes; then to embroidery or sewing buttons.	• Refinement of eye-hand coordination and grasp • To learn the practical skill of sewing • To practice precision and exactness
2+ years	Grading sizes of nuts and bolts	• Wooden board with various-sized holes • Nuts and bolts that fit into the holes in a container	• Eye-hand coordination
2+ years	Stretching elastic bands on a grid board	• Using a geoboard to stretch elastics—can create patterns or keep it open-ended	• Eye-hand coordination
2.5 years	Polishing shoes	• Container to hold 1. shoe polish (small amount) 2. finger mitt for applying polish 3. soft-bristled brush • Underlay that covers the whole table • Shoe horn, if outdoor shoes are worn	• Care of self
2.5+ years	Dressing frame: buckles	• Wooden frame, two pieces of leather fastened with three or four buckles • To practice buckles	• Care of self
2.5+ years	Helping with baking	• Help measure ingredients • Stir ingredients • Sweep and clean up after baking	• Food preparation
3+ years	Help unpack dishwasher	• Assist in emptying the dishwasher	• Daily life
3+ years	Help with recycling	• Sort recycling and bring it to container	• Daily life
3+ years	Make bed (pulling up a duvet)	• Make their own bed—duvet only	• Daily life
3+ years	Use toilet independently	• Have a step stool and a smaller toilet seat available or use a potty	• Daily life
3+ years	Assisting with more advanced cooking	• For example, helping to make lasagna	• Food preparation
3+ years	Feeding pets	• A small amount of fish food can be placed in an egg cup. • Getting water for dog • Giving food to cat, hamster, or other pet	• Daily life
3+ years	Help with folding laundry and socks	• Take part in the clothes-washing process • Invite child to sort items by person or color, pair socks, learn basic folding skills, and so on.	• Daily life
3+ years	Helping to get ready for visitors	• Making beds • Clearing spaces, picking up toys, and so on • Preparing meal	• Daily life
3+ years	First board games	• Orchard by HABA • Shopping list and other games by Orchard Toys • Simple card games, such as Snap • Games can be simplified, depending on the age of the child.	• Turn taking • Understanding simple rules • Fun

AGE	ACTIVITY NAME	DESCRIPTION/MATERIALS	AREA OF DEVELOPMENT
3+ years	More difficult sewing, arts and crafts materials	• Cards with more complicated shapes, like a heart • Sewing buttons • Sewing embroidery patterns • Sewing a cushion • Art projects with more than one step	• Art/self-expression
3+ years	Exploration of world around us	• For example, nature collections, birds, animals, plants, and trees	• Botany • Cultural studies • Life sciences
3+ years	More refined threading, sorting	• Shoelace with small beads • Piece of wool with small pieces of straw, using an embroidery needle	• Eye-hand coordination • Refining the grasp
3+ years	Composition puzzles—twelve or more pieces	• More difficult puzzles, including layered puzzles, composition puzzles, and puzzles with more pieces	• Refinement of eye-hand coordination and pincer grasp • Develops the ability to recognize a background shape
3+ years	Hammering shapes in corkboard	• Corkboard • Wooden shapes • Small nails and hammer	• Eye-hand coordination
3+ years	Pinprick work	• Shape drawn on paper to prick • Felt underlay • Pricking pen • The child follows along the line until the shape can be removed.	• Refinement of eye-hand coordination and grasp
3+ years	I spy	• If showing interest in sounds of letters, use phonetic sounds of letters.	• Language development • Prereading skills
3+ years	Calendar	• Make your own or buy a simple calendar in which the child can change the day, month, and weather. • Can add more details as the child gets older	• Time
3+ years	Lots of free play and outdoor play	• Allow time every day for the child to be outdoors and to have unstructured time to play.	• Daily life • Outdoor environment • Fun
3+ years	WEDGiTS	• WEDGiTS can be purchased; they allow building in sequence, and various patterns can be made.	• This is not a Montessori activity but would be suitable for the home environment.
3+ years	Well-selected building materials	• For example, Lego, Magna-Tiles, wooden blocks	• These are not Montessori activities but would be suitable for the home environment.
3+ years	Marble run	• There are beautiful wooden marble runs that children can build themselves.	• This is not a Montessori activity but would be suitable for the home environment.

INDEX

R

S

T

V

W

Y